Praise for *Let's Roll*

'Getting a tabletop gaming group up and running at your school or library can seem intimidating, particularly if you're an adult with little to no experience playing games like Dungeons & Dragons. Thankfully, in *Let's Roll*, Maxwell has done all the heavy lifting for you, clearly breaking down each step and even providing evidence and arguments should you need to get decision-makers at your school or library on board. Throughout the book, Maxwell's passion for tabletop gaming and his determination to make it accessible for everyone shine through. He writes with such heart that, by the time you turn the last page, you'll be ready to pick up your sword and jump into the fray!'
Alex Dunne, author of The Book of Secrets and halfling rogue

'A heartfelt and accessible guide, essential for beginners looking to easily introduce Dungeons & Dragons or other tabletop role-playing games to their library, community space or group of friends/family.

Let's Roll! is your helping hand to getting started, written through the real-life lens of Maxwell's experience: a librarian bringing joy and confidence to young people through collaborative gameplay and storytelling. This book presents a fantastic opportunity for compassion, personal growth and, of course, a whole lot of fun with friends old and new. If you've ever thought about running a TTRPG, you're in the right place!'
Alex 'Ally' Foulkes, D&D nerd and author of the Rules for Vampires series

'This is the book I've been looking for! So many teachers and other helping professionals dream of using TTRPGs with children, but imposter syndrome gets in the way: what if they don't have an encyclopedic knowledge of the rules, or the seemingly limitless creativity of a pro GM? Reading *Let's Roll* is like talking to a close friend who genuinely loves these games and wants you to love them, too. It's compassionate and beginner-friendly, but also takes a deep dive into the specific joys and challenges of running games with kids. I can't wait to start recommending it to others, it's a critical hit!'
Katie Lear, counsellor and founder of Young Dragonslayers

'Setting up a tabletop role-playing game in your library can feel like a daunting task, especially if you are an inexperienced player – the rules can appear overwhelming and the logistics prompt lots of questions. Lucas is the perfect guide to help you create a successful game; his warm and realistic advice takes into account the unique challenges librarians face and guides you from novice player to confident Dungeon Master! His passion for the proven benefits of playing TTRPGS with young people is infectious and inspiring. This book will be of great help to all librarians looking to join him in his quest to make these games accessible to all.'
Alice Leggatt, School Librarian

'*Let's Roll* is an essential guide for any person wanting to explore the wondrous world of D&D gameplay. Maxwell walks the reader through every aspect of the game of D&D with passion and clarity. He addresses every possible question that could be raised for a budding DM regarding the mechanics of game play, and demonstrates the incredible benefits so many students have experienced as a result of playing D&D. This book has been crafted with love and passion and will convince anyone to give D&D a try for themselves or their students.'

Gráinne O'Brien, founder of Rontu Literary Service and author of *A Limerick Fairytale*

'As a former teacher, an author specialising in kids' events and an avid fan of role-playing games, I cannot recommend this book highly enough. I've seen in person just how empowering RPGs can be for students but setting up and managing a sustainable group can be difficult.

In this, Maxwell's guide excels. It has everything you need: a perfect balance of meticulous detail and accessible, compassionate, student-forward design, all delivered with an enviable warmth and expertise. Every school should have a copy of this book.'

Dave Rudden, author of *Knights of the Borrowed Dark* and *Doctor Who*

Let's Roll

Every purchase of a Facet book helps to fund CILIP's advocacy, awareness and accreditation programmes for information professionals.

Let's Roll

A Guide to Setting up Tabletop Role-Playing Games in your School or Public Library

Lucas Maxwell

facet publishing

Published by Facet Publishing
c/o British Library, 96 Euston Road, London NW1 2DP
www.facetpublishing.co.uk

Facet Publishing is wholly owned by CILIP: the Library and Information Association.

British Library Cataloguing in Publication Data
A catalogue record for this book is available from the British Library.

ISBN 978-1-78330-613-8 (paperback)
ISBN 978-1-78330-614-5 (PDF)
ISBN 978-1-78330-615-2 (EPUB)

First published 2023

Typeset from author's files in 10.5/13pt University Old Style and Myriad Pro by Flagholme Publishing Services.
Printed and made in Great Britain by CPI Group (UK) Ltd, Croydon, CR0 4YY.

For Justine.

I could not have done this without you.

Contents

Figures

About the Author

Originally from Nova Scotia, Canada, Lucas Maxwell never dreamed he would become a librarian, but is very glad that he did. He fell in love with Dungeons & Dragons when he was nine years old when his brother gave him a battered copy of *Spellfire* by Ed Greenwood. He has been working with teens in public and school libraries for close to 15 years and is currently the librarian at Glenthorne High School in London, England. He writes for the literary website Book Riot and has contributed to the *School Library Journal* and American Library Association publications. In 2017 Lucas was named the School Librarian of the Year by the UK's School Library Association. In 2022 he won the Open University's Reading for Pleasure Teaching Award and the WriteMentor Novel in Development Award for his middle-grade contemporary novel *You Have Selected Power Drive*. His dream is to one day become an author in addition to being a librarian. He is currently the Dungeon Master for some amazing high school students and some equally amazing adults. He lives in Surrey, England, with his wife, two children and one always-hungry chocolate labrador.

Acknowledgements

There are many people to thank. First, I'd like to thank my wife for her endless support and love. I would not have been able to write this book without you. I'd also like to thank my children for being hilarious and very inspirational.

I'd like to thank my parents for their support and love – they have always been big cheerleaders of any project I've ever undertaken.

I couldn't go without thanking my brother Matt because he introduced me to the entire world of Dungeons & Dragons (D&D) when I was nine years old, when he handed me *Spellfire* by Ed Greenwood and *The Crystal Shard* by R. A. Salvatore. I hope you have found peace, buddy.

Big thanks to the D&D students at Glenthorne High School. There are too many of you to name, but you are amazing and hilarious and I thoroughly enjoy playing this awesome game with you in the library.

Thank you to Peter Baker at Facet Publishing for all of your advice and support in getting this idea off the ground. Thank you very much Alice Leggatt and Rebecca Strang, two amazing librarians who have provided invaluable feedback while I was writing this guide.

I'd also like to thank my D&D friends, some of whom I've never met in person but have made playing this game so much fun: Ian, Casey, Udi and Cae, thanks for helping me become a better GM and for the countless laughs over the years. And to my new friends, the cast of *You Should Have Been a Meat Shield*: Ally, Dave, Alex and Gráinne, thank you for adding to the thrill of being in this world and being so fun to talk to each week.

Glossary

Armour Class: The number that dictates how hard it is to hit you. For example, if your warrior has an Armour Class of 15, enemies must roll a 15 or higher on their attack rolls in order to do any damage.

AoE: Area of Effect. This typically refers to magic spells that affect a wide area rather than one specific creature.

Battle mat/map: A board or online board with hexes or squares to determine an area that players traverse. It does not necessarily have to be where battle takes place.

BBEG: Big Bad Evil Guy. This refers to the end boss or central villain in the story.

BTB: By the Book. *See* RAW.

D&D: Dungeons & Dragons

d20: A 20-sided die or dice.

Difficulty Check (DC): A number that a player must meet or exceed in order to achieve a particular goal. For example, a player wants to leap off the edge of a cliff and grab a rope. The DC for this action is 15. If the player rolls a 15 or higher - success! If they roll under 15, well, the GM gets to decide what happens next!

DM: Dungeon Master, also referred to as the Game Master. The person who organises, plans and delivers the game.

Dungeon Crawl: Refers to a specific kind of game where there is less role-playing and more exploring dungeons where a lot of combat takes place.

Experience points: Points that players accumulate in order to level up their characters.

Fudge: When a GM tells the players a different dice roll than what they actually rolled. For example, the GM rolls a 20 on an attack (usually considered a critical hit) but the GM knows that this will kill a player. Instead, the GM tells the player that they rolled a much lower number and survived.

Game Round Table RPG Guild: A Discord group that discusses tabletop role-playing games, offers support and much more.

GM: Game Master, also referred to as the Dungeon Master. The person who organises, plans and delivers the game.

Hex Crawl: A game where players explore large areas of a map, often travelling many miles to get from point A to point B.

Homebrew: A kind of adventure made entirely from the GM's head and not using pre-made adventures, characters or scenarios.

Hook: A prewritten part of a character's back story that ties it in with the overall story of the campaign.

HP: Hit Points. This number dictates your health in the game.

Initiative: How the GM determines the order that players take turns during combat.

Meat Shield: A player that can withstand a lot of damage and purposely blocks others from taking major damage so that they can perform other tasks or duties during combat.

Melee: Hand-to-hand combat, or close-quarters combat.

Milestone: An alternative to *Experience points* where players level up based on the quests they complete rather than being given a set number of points. These milestones can be determined by the GM. Example: 'You saved the villagers from the goblins and you found the child's missing puppy, that's enough to level up, welcome to level two!'

Minifig: A term used to describe a miniature figurine that represents a player, monster or character.

Nerf: To purposely reduce the power of an item or character ability in order to level the playing field.

NPC: Non-Player Character. A character typically greeted by the GM for the players to interact with or learn more from. In some instances, NPCs join the players on quests.

OoC: Out of Character. Players usually use this during online gaming where they step outside of their character's voice and use their own to talk about something non-game related or ask a specific question about the rules.

One Shot: An adventure that can be fully completed in one session.

OP: Over Powered, typically referring to a weapon or ability that other players feel gives a player unfair advantage over other things in the game.

PvP: Player versus Player.

RAW: Rules as Written. Refers to following the rules exactly as they are written in the book.

RP: Roleplay

RPG: Role-Playing Game

Rule of Cool: When a player does something unorthodox and slightly bends the rules but it makes for a memorable experience and the GM allows it.

Rule Zero: The idea that the GM has final say on all rulings despite what the rule book says.

Sandbox: When players appear to have absolute freedom of movement. The GM provides multiple routes, places and quests and allows the players to choose where they want to go and what they want to do.

Session Zero: A session you have with your players before you actually play the game. This is a session aimed at character creation, setting the ground rules and ensuring everyone is on board with what style of game they are going to play.

Tank: A player that is very tough, strong and able to withstand a lot of damage before succumbing.

Theatre of the Mind (ToTM): When you play a tabletop role-playing game and don't use maps or miniature figures, you and your players simply imagine what is happening.

TPK: Total Party Kill

TTRPG: Tabletop Role-playing Game

XP: *see* Experience Points

Introduction

The library tables were pushed together, eight teens crammed around them. In front of them lay character sheets, snacks, dice, notes, illustrations and more snacks.

One player, a wizard, had found a wand and decided to cast it on an enemy they had encountered in a haunted amusement park. 'I use my wand to kill this evil dude!' he yelled. The wand was powerful but the power came with a cost, there was a chance that it would fail and sometimes a random negative effect would take place. This was one of those times.

Instead of sending an arc of blue lightning to kill the enemy, it exploded in the wizard's face in a cloud of pink dust. Almost immediately, all of his character's hair fell out and landed on the ground at his feet. 'I love this game so much!' he shouted in between fits of cry/laughter.

Playing Tabletop Role-playing Games (TTRPGs) in my school library has changed my life. I do not say this lightly. It truly has been a form of therapy for me. Whatever type of TTRPG you decide to play, whatever number of students you can bring in, your goal should be to have a moment like the one described above.

Thank you for purchasing this guide! I really hope you find it useful. Why have I written a book helping librarians to run TTRPGs? One of the main reasons is that they can be a huge amount of fun. In fact, this would be my number one rule: to have fun. If you aren't having fun with your players, you will need to ask yourself or your players why this is. Yes, the games can be chaotic and sometimes feel slightly unhinged, but if you organise yourself and do a little preparation, the sessions will be very beneficial.

The games, activities and events that I will discuss in this book are meant to be a catharsis. I want to share the research and discussions I've had with other people from around the world in regard to the benefits you can take away from playing TTRPGs.

Another reason I wanted to write this book is that I genuinely feel they can act as a form of therapy for both you and the youth you serve. I am not a psychologist, so I'm not qualified to say what the actual impact is, but I know it has helped me a great deal.

That said, I have spoken to medical professionals, other librarians and players themselves about these benefits and I want to ensure that public and school librarians understand how great TTRPGs can be. Yes, they are games, but there is a tangible mental health and well-being benefit to them. I know this because I benefit greatly from them myself. TTRPGs are a form of therapy. You might think to yourself, 'Well, I'm just playing a game,' but as this book will explore, there is a lot of research to prove how therapeutic this can be.

I also wrote this book because when I first approached TTRPGs I felt a huge amount of anxiety. The scope of the games simply felt too massive: I was overwhelmed by all of the rules and I was paranoid that I was missing something crucial. This stopped me from becoming a GM (Game Master), not only in the school where I work but in my personal life as well. I felt like I wouldn't live up to the GMs I was watching on YouTube.

The truth is, you never have to live up to those people. They are amazing, yes, but they are amazing for different reasons. They are usually professional actors or get to play TTRPGs for a living. I wish I could play games like this for a living, but for 99.9% of us it's a hobby that we get to do in the extremely little free time we have.

Therefore, this book is also here to tell you not to be hard on yourself. If you and the students or teens you work with are having fun, that is all that you need to worry about.

One thing that helped ease my anxiety around running a TTRPG was learning about the 'rule of cool', which essentially means that you as a GM can allow things to happen that bring fun and excitement to the table even if they bend the rules. In this light, I realised that it didn't matter if I forgot the intricacies of every rule. Is everyone having fun and laughing together as a team? If the answer is yes, then I carry on the way I was.

By the same token, I hope this book helps to bring some clarity to public and school librarians, and also teachers, who really want to try a TTRPG in their school but are feeling that same sense of anxiety that I did.

This book will also offer alternatives to the big names in the TTRPG world. For example, many librarians might be considering starting a Dungeons & Dragons (D&D) programme in their public or school library. I currently run D&D and it is a lot of fun, but it does take a lot of time and effort. Therefore, in my opinion, if you are going to run D&D, you have to love it yourself and have some extra time on your hands, otherwise I really feel it will fall apart.

Luckily, for anyone who feels like they don't have the time to pour into creating a D&D environment in their library, there are dozens of alternatives out there. I mention these and describe them in more detail in Chapter 5. The bottom line is that these will save you hours of time, they are light on rules and are aimed at younger audiences than traditional TTRPGs like D&D.

The other thing I know is that these games are unique to any other programme I've ever run in a library for over 15 years. The reason it's unique? The students *never* miss a session. When I run manga club, book club, film club, mock trial, maker space or any of the other clubs in our library, students come and go, they have other commitments or they lose interest. This is the only programme where this has not happened. The same six students who started playing this game with me in November 2020 are still with me as I write this nearly two years later. It has also gained many more students, and I will explain how I organise the programme in Chapter 1.

This is why TTRPGs are unique and why I hope this guide will be helpful in getting you started.

Who am I?

I am currently the school librarian at Glenthorne High School in Sutton, Surrey, England. I have been in this position since 2013. Before that I was the Teen Services Librarian at Halifax Public Libraries in Nova Scotia, Canada, where I'm originally from.

When I was in the fourth grade our teacher read *The Hobbit* out loud to us, and it changed my life. I couldn't believe a book like that even existed. I immediately asked to be given *The Lord of the Rings*, but didn't actually tackle reading it until much later.

Around this time, my brother introduced me to D&D, specifically the book series surrounding the fantastic character Drizzt Do'Urden and his friends Breunor and Wulfgar. I was hooked. I loved every aspect of it. I got the game Hero Quest for Christmas and wore it out. I got stacks of graph paper from school and made my own dungeons, complete with back stories and filled with demons and monsters.

That said, I actually played a very limited amount of the tabletop version of D&D in the mid- to late 1980s. This was the era of Advanced D&D 2nd edition. Growing up in a very rural area of Canada, I found it hard to find people who wanted to play and there was no internet, so I read the *Forgotten Realms* book series and played D&D games on my Tandy 1000 home computer. These were games like Champions of Krynn and Eye of the Beholder. These were the things that kept TTRPGs in my mind as I grew up. In my teens I got out of TTRPGs until I discovered computer games like Everquest, when I was in my early twenties. Therefore, I never really felt that I stopped being in love with TTRPGs; I just didn't realise how much of an impact these types of games and novels had on me. Then, when I was in my early forties, I was diagnosed as autistic. This came as both a huge shock to me and not a shock at the same time. I was able to piece things together in my life and I slowly realised that TTRPGs like D&D were my special interest as an autistic person. I just didn't know it before. I can talk about these kinds of games for hours, I can create multiple NPC (Non-Player Characters) with fully fledged backstories, I can regale others with my characters' exploits, to either their amusement or confusion. To make a long story short, TTRPGs have been hugely important in my life and have acted as a form of therapy for me, and continue to do so.

How I started a TTRPG in my library

Pre-COVID, I ran D&D mostly through the massive popularity of the horror sci-fi TV programme *Stranger Things*. I surveyed the students and asked them if they would enjoy starting a TTRPG in the library. The response was overwhelming: the students were very interested in starting one.

I spent roughly £14 (USD17) to get things started. At the time, it was entirely student led. You may find this works best for your space, considering the amount of time you have available. During this time I had two students who knew TTRPGs well and could act as the GM without a lot of guidance from me.

In all honesty, at that time I felt somewhat overwhelmed by the world of TTRPGs and I did not have enough time to invest. My advice is to seek out older, more mature students to lead a TTRPG if you do not have the time to invest in it yourself. In Chapter 4, I provide step-by-step instructions on how to help a teen become a great GM.

Just prior to the COVID lockdown in March 2020, the students who were acting as GM had new commitments that meant they could no longer take part in running the sessions. The need was definitely still there, and so I decided to try to take over and become GM. It's not as hard as it seems. Yes, it can feel overwhelming, but it doesn't have to be. I will provide more tips and hints on this in Chapter 4.

When the country went into lockdown, I assumed that playing TTRPGs was all over for the time being. It turned out that it was only getting started. Our school used Microsoft Teams to run virtual lessons throughout the lockdown, and so I decided to use Teams to run our TTRPG sessions. It was a huge success, and it also meant that we could run it almost every single day either at lunch times or after school, mainly because the students did not have anywhere to go, and neither did I.

It was a lot of fun and hugely therapeutic for me mentally during a stressful time. I feel that it was also the same for the students as they never missed a session. These same students are still playing twice weekly with me and haven't missed a session in a very long time.

When we went into our first lockdown here in the UK, I also started to play D&D with my son. Looking back, it was a way to reduce anxiety that we both had. The first lockdown was very strict and there were a lot of unanswered questions circulating, so it became a way to ease our anxiety, and because I had more time on my hands I started to get excited about it. I bought all the books and dove straight in. I will discuss what you need to play TTRPGs in Chapter 3, and I want to assure you that you do not have to spend a lot of money to play.

We came out of lockdown and I almost immediately had students asking if we could start up again, and this time I felt more confident in running the group so I decided that I would take more control over it and take on permanent GM duties.

I think that if you ask the students or teens in your library, you will find that yes, they are very interested in starting or creating a TTRPG club in your library.

How to use the book

This book is not necessarily meant to be read from beginning to end. Instead, you may find that you are already at a certain stage at setting up a TTRPG programme in your school or public library. This section will give a brief summary of each chapter so that you can determine which one is right for you to get started with.

Chapter 1 focuses both on attracting players to the game and on convincing the powers that be that running a TTRPG is a good idea. This might not be an issue for you. It wasn't for me, but things always change, so it's important to know effective ways to promote the games and to bring in interested students. The chapter also covers proposals for convincing line managers and senior leaderships to be on board with the programme. I also discuss the mental health and well-being benefits of playing TTRPGs in the library. All of these put together make for an amazing package to bring to your senior leadership or management team so they can be made aware of the benefits. Unfortunately, it's easy for many to view these as frivolous uses of a librarian's time, but as drama therapist Katie Lear says, 'every time you play, you are engaging in therapy for these kids'.

Chapter 2 consists of five case studies from librarians around the world, focusing on how they set up their TTRPGs, the benefits they see from them, any issues that arise and how they pitched their programmes to senior leadership and management. The chapter also provides an example TTRPG proposal for you to use if you need it.

Chapter 3 provides step-by-step instructions on how to start a TTRPG in your school or public library. The chapter covers promotion, ways to keep the game moving and ways that will help you avoid the game becoming mired down. Sometimes when this happens it can cause a lot of disruption and you find that your entire time spent planning the session has been lost to something that could have been cleared up quickly. There are several tricks and tips that can be applied to ensure that your players aren't getting bored or too distracted. There is a fine balance between enforcing rules at the table and making sure everyone is having fun. I think that if you use the right TTRPGs (see Chapter 5), then you will be one step ahead of the game.

Chapter 4 covers what is called Session Zero. This a session (or multiple sessions) that can take place in person or even over a series of e-mails that will help students to understand what kind of game they are getting involved in. This will be especially helpful for them if they are completely new to the game or if you yourself are fairly new to it. In my opinion, holding a Session Zero will help to remove any ambiguity and establish clear rules about the game. This is an important chapter because Session Zero can be as involved or as quick as you want it to be. My advice is to take your time and get to know your players a little bit before launching in, especially if you are running a longer campaign in a TTRPG like Quest or D&D (see Chapter 5 for an in-depth exploration of TTRPGs like Quest).

Chapter 5 comprises four things. First, there is a list and review of 20 great TTRPGs that you can have in your library. All TTRPGs require you to roll dice; sometimes these are multi-sided, sometimes they are standard, six-sided dice. Each review in the chapter contains information on what kind of dice are required. The chapter then provides links to online resources and a further reading list, as well as a list of fiction books for children aged 9+.

I hope you enjoy reading this book, and I hope you will feel confident enough to start your own TTRPG in the library after reading it. Good luck, and let's roll!

1 Convincing the Powers that Be

Introduction

You've got an idea to play a TTRPG in your school or public library, you know your students or patrons want to be engaged, but you need buy-in from senior leadership, your manager or both. You might also need a budget to bring in the games, books, dice, food, whatever you think will make your gaming session a success. This chapter will deal with evidence to show managers and senior leadership why running a TTRPG in your library is a good idea.

As I mentioned in the Introduction, the number one rule you should follow when playing a TTRPG in your school or public library is to have fun. There is more to this than just a word, though. The idea of fun carries with it a lot of weight, today more than ever. Preston (2020) states that the concept of playing and having fun can have significant benefits for learning such as retaining information and being open to new ideas, for example. When someone is attempting to create something and becomes stuck, they will often abandon the framework of rules that they've been given and daydream, says Preston (2020). And in schools, assignments and programmes that incorporate playing will hold students' attention for longer.

TTRPGs can be considered playing just for fun, but, as this chapter will explore, the games are much deeper than that and have many benefits. I have spoken to many teens about why they love playing TTRPGs in our library. One of the main reasons they enjoy it is that it carries with it a certain freedom to explore with their friends. The GM has created a world and they are able to exist within it as they want, with no judgement.

Why collect TTRPGs?

If you are hoping to collect TTRPGs and start a programme in a school or public library, you will be filling a public need. Like the programme or not (and I haven't met anyone who *doesn't* like it), *Stranger Things* has, in my opinion, catapulted TTRPGs like D&D into a new realm. I have spoken to both public and school librarians who have said this is the number one thing on their young patrons' minds when asking about playing a TTRPG: I'm going to be playing the same game as my heroes on *Stranger Things*.

When you collect TTRPGs, you will attract new users and faces to your library. Forsythe (2019, 6) states that having a strong TTRPG collection will encourage players to use the existing library collection, considering that most TTPRGs are rooted in mythology, ancient cultures and medieval settings. This applies to collections in both public and school libraries.

I have personally used TTRPGs to highlight specific parts of the school library's collection, such as our 'Choose Your Own Adventure' section, which is heavily based in mythology and fantasy. Other areas of the collection that I've connected with are our myths and legends books and our comic book and manga collection, specifically *Amulet*, *Lightfall* and *Delicious in Dungeon*, to name just a few.

There are opportunities in both public and school libraries to create book displays (Figure 1.1), run different programmes and tie books into your TTRPG setting. To give an example of this, our student D&D team in the school library where I work were very fortunate to meet author

Figure 1.1 *Library display featuring Dungeons & Dragons*

Kimberley Pauley, who writes campaigns for D&D's 5th edition games. When I reached out to her and explained the popularity of the game with our students she went above and beyond and allowed them to become official play testers for a new campaign she was writing. When she visited, she spent over three hours with the students, running the campaign and going over the setting and the world. It was a tremendous moment for me, and I know the students really enjoyed it as well.

Another example is our library Comic Con (comic book convention), which we run every year on a Saturday. In one of our recent Comic Cons, the majority of the students who came were TTRPG fans and simply wanted to play D&D. This has prompted me to plan for a 'Dungeon Con' event where we will have guest GMs and 50 students playing the same TTRPG at different tables all at once. All of this would not be possible if we weren't collecting TTRPGs in the library.

It is also important, when you do decide to collect TTRPGs in your library, that you explore a variety of genres. This will help to ensure that you are meeting the likes and tastes of as many library users as possible. There are several different kinds of TTRPGs out there, which reach into fantasy, science fiction, horror and fables. Chapter 5 has a list of 20 TTRPGs that span many different genres.

By running a TTRPG in your school or public library you will do many things: you will bring new faces into the library, increase book circulation and, of course, increase footfall. You will do more than that, however, because it will create an atmosphere of acceptance, creativity and pure bliss. Those are very important goals for any librarian. In my library, D&D has brought in several new students who have become library regulars. They borrow books, they engage with others in a positive way – and there is a lot of evidence out there to show that these games provide huge benefits to students in terms of mental health and well-being.

Benefits to literacy

As a school librarian, I am constantly trying to put books into the hands of every student who walks through the door, but especially those who tell me they hate reading. It can be disheartening, frustrating and demoralising to hear this over and over again. In my experience, TTRPGs are perfectly geared towards students who claim they don't like to read.

This is because if they want to engage and play the game, they will be reading a ton of material. I have students who come to the library twice weekly for library lessons. Finding a book for some of them is extremely difficult. They tell me reading is boring, they tell me they aren't interested in anything and they tell me that they don't have any time to read.

The same students who have told me this but have engaged in TTRPGs end up reading without even knowing it. They are poring over the handbooks, the rule books, the monster books. They are researching backstories online, they are sitting around with their friends after school, reading about the deadliest creatures that can be fought and the most sought-after treasure. Yet, they will still tell me they don't like to read. It's a perfect way to get them reading and engaged and involved in a positive environment with their friends.

I've been working with youth in libraries for nearly 15 years, and one thing that stands out above everything else is that they want choice. Youth who use libraries do not want to be told what to read. This is why they tend to go for material that is often not recommended by adults, even teachers and other librarians. This includes comic books, manga and other reading material that is considered 'lesser' or not so important. TTRPGs fall into this category because they are often an enigma to the general population. Some adults may remember the fast-lived yet devastating 'Satanic panic' in the 1980s where large American news outlets portrayed games like D&D as actual portals to hell. I was also banned from playing D&D for a short time by my parents who thought it would drive me to suicide (a popular view among parents at that time).

For many kids, TTRPGs are something that exist on the edge. TV shows such as *Stranger Things* have propelled them into the mainstream, but they will always attract those who feel a little left out by society, a little on the fringe of what is considered cool or not cool by the student body. This is why collecting TTRPGs in your library is so important: they will bring in these kids, who will check out the books you have to offer and will then tell their friends – and then you will have an amazing story to tell, because your TTRPG programme will be brimming with life.

In a study conducted at the University of Northern Iowa in 2017, all participants who engaged in TTRPGs cited at least one literacy skill that had been positively affected (Kaylor, 2017, 21). These skills included reading, writing, speaking and listening.

One participant, who was dyslexic, stated that his love for TTRPGs like D&D motivated him to read the rule book, which improved his reading skills. Another participant stated how much they recommended D&D to improve writing skills. In their words, 'I'd definitely recommend D&D at writers looking at how to understand characters and to understand how to craft an effective story' (Kaylor, 2017, 23).

Bringing in TTRPGs into the library, and therefore to the community in which librarians serve, encourages co-operation, improved speaking skills and a high level of reading for pleasure (Kaylor, 2017, 32). The evidence is there that TTRPGs help to build friendships, improve reading and public-speaking skills and foster a desire to be creative.

Hutton (2017, as cited in Forsythe, 2019, 4) also discusses how TTRPGs are very helpful when it comes to reading comprehension and critical-thinking skills. The games deal with listening skills, and players need to visualise in their minds what the GM is narrating. The players need to pay attention to how other characters react to different situations. They then need to develop their own clever strategies to overcome obstacles.

This is one reason why setting ground rules at the beginning is so important. It is crucial that players pay attention to what is going on in order for them to get the most out of the game. Rules around your table are discussed in Chapter 4.

In addition to improving literacy, there is concrete evidence to show that TTRPGs can actually provide moral training for young adults. In a study conducted in 2017 at a college in Charleston, South Carolina, Wright, Weissglass and Casey (2017) found that young adults who spent time playing D&D displayed significant growth in moral development, compared to young adults who did not play the games. Wright, Weissglass and Casey state that their study showed that games like D&D can act as an interactive moral training ground.

For example, a session in my school library with teens once devolved into a scene where one player decided they would torture an NPC (a Non-Player Character that I had created for them to interact with). In this case, the NPC was a villain and was trying to sabotage them. The players discovered this, and one player decided it was torture time. This was almost immediately stamped out by the other players, who were clearly uncomfortable with this kind of behaviour. I have run over 300 TTRPG sessions with teens in both public and school libraries and this was the only time something that like this came up. What I have seen are players who are genuinely concerned for these NPCs, players who look out for each other (albeit with a lot of gentle ribbing) and players who want to do the right thing when given a moral dilemma.

TTRPGs are a form of catharsis for students and adults alike, but there is much more to it than that. TTRPGs like D&D can teach students empathy and social skills (King, 2021). Mental health professionals are also using them to help autistic children to develop appropriate forms of communication and learn how to create friendships and develop social skills in a safe and fun environment (King, 2021). In my own experience, I see students who are normally shy, introverted and even withdrawn use TTRPGs to come out of their shell, develop strong friendship circles and communicate in ways I hadn't seen them do previously. This includes creating artistic impressions of their campaigns and characters as well as writing backstories and character arcs.

TTRPGs such as D&D can also help to treat anxiety and depression and can become a crucial social outlet. We saw this during lockdowns: the loneliness that is attributed to staying home for long periods of time can have a huge impact on anyone's mental health and well-being. Playing D&D and other TTRPGs can be an effective remedy for this, as it gives people something to look forward to every time they play, and allows players to embark on exciting adventures with friends, some new, some old, without having to leave home (King, 2021).

There is further evidence to show that TTRPGs can help in developing language skills. Snow (2019) states that he runs a D&D club in his high school library, where most of the players are Spanish speaking. One player in particular struggled with English, so the GM simply made Elvish (what her character spoke) Spanish so she that could express herself in the game. Phrases spoken in Elvish were then translated by another student who knew both Elvish and Common (English). In this unique way, the GM helped the player to learn English while she played and, in turn, helped the other players learn Spanish. Snow states that the last thing he wants is for any student to think they cannot play because of a language barrier. TTRPGs are for everyone, and carry with them tangible benefits.

Benefits to mental health and well-being

In running TTRPGs in my library over a period of three years, I have seen at first hand the positive impact of these games. I've seen introverted, shy students join groups to play flamboyant characters and I've seen friendship circles form and grow.

I've also heard from the students themselves. Here are a few quotes from them on the benefits of playing D&D in the library:

> D&D is the best part of my day, it helps remove all of the bad feelings that I've had recently.
>
> (15-year-old student)

> I love D&D because it's fun having adventures together, I love the setting and the danger, it's a lot of fun.
>
> (15-year-old student)

> I love the tranquillity, peace and freedom of D&D in the library!
>
> (13-year-old student)

I love D&D as it offers escape but also the opportunity to be more free because of the lack of judgement people have – characters can be weird and wacky in any way and nobody even blinks an eye! Plus our group in the library is definitely a safe space for me.

(15-year-old student)

D&D is an amazing game that can take your mind off everyday problems and take you into a whole new world. Since you can do almost anything, there's a lot of options where the campaign can go. It is also nice to socialise with other people who have the same interests.

(13-year-old student)

I know that this game has had a real impact, but I wanted to speak to a medical professional who could substantiate what I was seeing and what the students were relating to me. That is why I interviewed Katie Lear, a Drama Therapist and Mental Health Counsellor in the United States. Katie runs a very successful TTRPG therapy programme for youth. After speaking to her, I discovered some very interesting insights into the world of D&D and TTRPGs in general.

Lear (2022) states that, no matter what kind of drama exists in the outside world, students can use TTRPGs like D&D to forget about it for a while and engage in a fun, safe activity that connects them with other like-minded people. This echoes a lot of what the students have said to me over the last few years and what I've been witnessing.

There are many reasons why TTRPGs work so well in therapy sessions. One is that the concept of 'play' is inherently therapeutic, and structured fun activities have huge benefits. Many students and even adults do not have the kinds of enriching experiences that can come from therapeutic play. In school, particularly high school, the focus is often on exams and exam preparation. Yes, extra-curricular activities are offered but often these fall by the wayside as homework, studying and revision take over. These are important aspects of high school life, but there needs to be a balance. TTRPGs provide this balance and more, because they act as a form of therapy for the students and the adults running them.

Lear (2022) also discussed the concept of Behaviour Activation. Behaviour Activation is a technique that is used to treat depression. Depression can be (among many things) caused by the absence of things to look forward to. Many students, especially during the pandemic, have lost a lot of extra-curricular activities. The resulting feeling of emptiness has, tragically, carried over in the minds of both students and adults alike, even after the return to 'normal' situations at home, work and school.

Playing TTRPGs means that you are having a scheduled event where you are essentially writing in the calendar that you are going to have fun. It is social, it is creative and there is a real sense of satisfaction from achieving your goals. I firmly believe that this is why the students never miss a session in the library. They have scheduled it into their lives, they are experiencing the benefits, and are having fun and don't want to miss out.

Another important benefit of TTRPGs is the concept of Role Theory. Lear (2022) states that some people can become stuck in rigid ways of presenting themselves to the world. This can limit the way we interact with others and prevents us from experiencing different ideas, emotions and, therefore, the benefits that come with these.

Playing TTRPGs lets us try out many different ways of being; it allows us to place ourselves in the shoes of different races, cultures and even creatures. We can experience a different way of being with no real-life consequences. What then happens, and what therapists are witnessing, is that youth who engage in TTRPGs use these broader ways of being in the outside world in positive ways once they get comfortable with practising them in the game.

Lear (2022) also walked me through a typical D&D therapy session. A D&D therapy session is fully immersed within the game. Therapy sessions ensure that the game feels safe; for example, you are not allowed to play a character whose personality is there simply to disrupt or to attack the other characters. I will discuss more about setting up rules that ensure everyone feels safe in Chapter 3.

In addition, during a therapy session players are not able to critique the other players' choices. You need to give players permission to make mistakes in the game. Therapists will ask if there are any triggering concepts, or any things that you hope the players will want to avoid. This may require a more one-to-one conversation with some players, but it's important to establish early on, says Lear.

Therapists will work with GMs to ensure that specific areas of support are brought into the game. An example is a player who had real issues with public speaking or organising their thoughts. The therapist asked the student if they wanted their character to deliver a speech in the game. They were given time to construct and prepare the speech and created a situation that came across as spontaneous.

I have also witnessed this kind of involvement in the library: students who are not comfortable speaking publicly eventually have spoken at length about how they are going to solve a puzzle, help their fallen comrades or defeat a hideous monster. I have personally been surprised on more than one occasion when I see this happen. I'll think 'Wow, I don't think I've heard them speak for so long!' All this happens in a positive, safe environment without judgement.

Another important aspect of therapy sessions is inspiration points (points that characters can 'spend' to give them a better chance of succeeding). For example, a character tries to leap over a chasm, they roll terribly and will fall to their death because of this. However, if they have in the past been awarded an inspiration point they can ask the GM if they can spend that point and reroll their chance to jump over the chasm. Inspiration points are awarded to players who do good deeds within the game, such as helping another character out, being overly nice to an NPC who requires assistance or doing something selfless that benefits the group as a whole. I love this idea and am going to implement it more often in my games.

In my experience, TTRPGs help to develop strong empathy skills and bring a closeness to the group that I haven't experienced before. A game that is reviewed in Chapter 5, called No Thank You, Evil!, has a system in place which is amazing for younger players. The aim of the game is to help others, not harm or hurt anyone. If you feel your players would benefit from a system like this, I strongly recommend checking it out.

Lear (2022) also states that it's important that the therapists don't impose their will too much on the players, as the players will get annoyed with this. TTRPGs in general are collaborative events. These are not games where you are fighting your friends. You and your friends must come together to fight a common enemy.

Working together is crucial. The creative freedom that TTRPGs offer is truly amazing. There aren't many board or video games that allow you to customise your character and your world in any way that you see fit.

Here is an example: I am the GM in my school library with teens and I also GM a TTRPG for adults once a week. I have students who have made a robot lumberjack, a teen vampire that gets extra powers if she plays her guitar well enough, a penguin warrior that can deliver a ferocious slide attack and even a rogue anteater that pickpockets using her tongue. I couldn't make that previous sentence up very easily, but give players the freedom to do what they want, and they will surprise and delight you every time.

Benefits of TTRPGs for autistic players

I will start by saying that I am not a medical professional. I am, however, autistic and can speak from a genuine place when it comes to the benefits of playing a game like D&D. I have spoken to other librarians, and one has stated that 80% of her D&D players at her school library were neurodiverse and she has seen all of the benefits listed below.

Controlled chaos

I struggle with organisation and feeling overwhelmed. For me, D&D creates a world in which there is chaos, but it is carefully controlled. Yes, the game can be overwhelming in terms of scope and grasping the rules, but once you're in you realise that nobody knows all of the rules and you don't have to. The enjoyment is in exploring and looking things up when fun, strange or hilarious events happen. And if you make a mistake and accidentally break the rules, so what? There are no real-life consequences; your character might have suffered for it, but that's all.

In addition, the simple act of creating a character is therapeutic for me. I have spoken with our teen players about this, one of whom told me they create characters when they're bored or feeling anxious. It's a methodical, exploratory researching process that has a lot of open ends to it, yet you know that you can pick away at it in your own time. There's no real deadline crunch, no one is going to be upset with you if you don't have your character made or if you're simply messing around with the handbook and diving into your own world.

Communication

Another thing I struggle with is communication. I do not enjoy looking people in the eye or meeting one to one. I find small talk excruciatingly uncomfortable. However, being in a small group that has a common purpose – and a made-up one at that – helps me to communicate with others in a way that I've never experienced before. The game requires communication; there is no way around it: it requires teamwork. In a school or employment setting, I'd rather have my fingernails pulled out than be put into a team to do a 'life building' exercise. With D&D, I cannot wait to be part of the team – even as the GM, I'm part of the team. Your job as GM is not to kill the other players, it's to create a world where they can have fun, be challenged and create their own stories.

I am often speaking through my character or, as a GM, speaking through multiple NPCs that the team meets. I can also create a world as a GM that challenges the players while telling an interesting, fun or strange story.

I really love this. I can spend hours creating NPCs and developing their personalities, and enjoy watching players interact with them. I found that as a normally shy person I could actually do voices and get into scenes and characters while in D&D and then, when out of D&D, boom! I'm back to that awkward introvert that mumbles and shies away from conversation.

Games like D&D are also amazing ways for autistic people to begin conversations. This might sound strange to some people but for me, simply understanding how to start a conversation can be tricky. However, with a head full of D&D information, stats, stories and experiences, I can easily and immediately connect with other players. This does not need to be D&D exclusive, it can be related to other things, but using D&D as a 'way in' is very useful.

Community

I am in no way hoping to turn this into a pity party, but the truth is that I have struggled with maintaining friendships my entire life. There are a couple of reasons for this. I tire easily, as do many autistic people. This is because we have to mask all day long to fit into what we perceive as 'normal' society, and this is mentally draining. Therefore I've never really had the patience or energy to develop real friendships – and when some do come along, I am often too self-absorbed to notice, or there is a miscommunication and I am perceived as stubborn or stand-offish.

With D&D, I am part of a built-in community. We are all there for one common purpose: we love the game and we love playing in the world that has been created. There is no awkwardness or social cues to worry about, in my experience, because through the game I've created great friendships; without the game I wouldn't have had these connections. As someone who would normally shy away from parties or social events, D&D has become my social event or my party (no pun intended). There's no small talk needed since we all want to get down to business and have fun, roll some dice, slay some monsters, find some loot and build a story together. It's a very unique situation, in my experience.

Empathy and understanding

Despite several stereotypes, an autistic person can be as empathetic as anyone. What happens, as I see it, is that people perceive us to lack empathy because of the possibility of blank facial expressions, or special interests that can override other people's feelings at times. I cannot tell you how many times I've been asked 'what's wrong?' or 'you look exhausted' (I probably am, and please don't say this to people) based solely on my facial expression. I used to have a joke that said my resting face was existential terror. Some people don't know how to react to it or assume I am angry or checked out, when the truth is I am probably very tired from coping all day long or thinking about something that I find interesting.

D&D teaches a lot of things, and one of them is waiting your turn and being respectful of others, something that our teens playing D&D have ten-fold, in my experience. You are literally putting yourself in someone else's shoes: a new race, sometimes not even a human being. You have to think from their perspective: how might they perceive the world? You also must be respectful of your teammates' stories, goals and dreams. As shy and introverted as I am, I also can cut people off mid-sentence, or they assume that I'm not interested because I won't make eye contact. With D&D I know I'm in a world where the other players' stories are important and need to be worked out and listened to. On a base level, their stories are also crucial to my own survival within the game, therefore it is in my interest to help their characters as much as possible.

D&D has been a real bridge for me to connect, have fun and engage more in the outside world. Again, this is only from my perspective: there are medical professionals out there who discuss more broadly the benefits that tabletop role playing has for mental health and general well-being.

Artistic freedom

As mentioned, there really is no limit to games like D&D. For instance, if you enjoy drawing maps (something I discovered that I really do enjoy) and using them to create towns, cities, dark lairs filled with bad guys, a TTRPG is a perfect escape. You might also want to draw your character, or describe their background and history in great detail. I have many students in the library who visit before school and during break and lunch times simply to bring out their character sheets and discuss them with their D&D friends. Yes, many of these students have been diagnosed as autistic and they are fully immersed in the game.

On the flip side of this, there are defined rules. These are the framework from which you deliver the game. The rules are extremely comforting to someone like me because, yes, I may have created a world with limitless possibilities that players can explore, but the way they explore that world and how they interact with different people or objects and the way their character fights has clearly defined rules. I can be a very 'black and white' type of person, and although there is a lot of grey area in games like D&D, these are typically in situations that are quickly resolved by the GM or the players themselves. If you have a monster with an Armor Class of 19 and a player rolls a 15 to try and hit it, the rules clearly say that this is a miss because they did not match or exceed the monster's Armor Class. These are the kinds of rules that lower my anxiety, because they will always be there. Every TTRPG you play will have a set of core rules that are essential. For an autistic player, in that they provide a springboard for participation, that helps a great deal.

Oxendine (2022), too, writes that being autistic means he struggles with conversations, yet with TTRPGs like D&D he feels more in control and more comfortable. This is because the social rules of the game are all written down. The dice determine what's going to happen and the GM has the ability to create a world that players can explore using said dice. It not only provides a framework for how to interact with people (Oxendine, 2022), but you as GM are creating the framework. As Oxendine puts it, 'It's much harder to get lost in a maze that you helped create'.

Many autistic people like myself practise conversations in their head when they know they've got one approaching. This is exhausting in many ways, but in a TTRPG it can help because it means you have a bank of interactions in your head that can be translated over to the game - at least, it does for me.

Even further, famous D&D dungeon master (DM) and guide Mike Shea states that he's never happier than when he's playing D&D with his friends and family (Shea, 2019). This is because it can be hard to make adult friends, and when we do connect with adults, there is a limit to what you can discuss - work, kids, politics (ha ha!!), the weather and so on. Finding a specific context like TTRPGs removes all of the awkwardness, and awkwardness is not something that only high school kids deal with - adults deal with it every day.

Having a scheduled time for you and your friends to hang out and immerse yourselves in another world as rich and open as TTRPGs can change your entire perspective (Shea, 2019). This is the same for teens; awkwardness is rife, and it can be hard for many of them to feel like they belong. For many, a school library can be their only safe haven in their school, and possibly in their lives.

If you add a TTRPG to the mix, what you are doing is giving many of these teens a way to connect socially with others that they may not have experienced before. Engaging in games like D&D can make you happier. This is because what makes you happy isn't fame or money, it's family, friends and real connections, it's building positive relationships in our lives (Shea, 2019). When a teen in the library tells me that D&D 'is the best part of coming to school', and another student who graduated in June still comes in to play and engage with the other students in their campaign, I know I've hit on something. I know there is some reason why they are coming back time and time again.

Summary

So, to recap, here is a condensed version of the above, in case you want to bring this to your management team but don't want them to have to read 6,000 words.

There is significant evidence to demonstrate that these games:

- have a positive impact on literacy;
- can act as moral training grounds;
- help to boost mental health and well-being;
- improve empathy and understanding;
- help to build a framework for how to interact positively with others;
- greatly help autistic youth in several social and communicative ways;
- increase library footfall;
- increase library book circulation with tie-ins and author visits;
- create an atmosphere that is safe, understanding and fun.

2 Case Studies

Introduction

This chapter contains case studies from five librarians in different settings and areas of the world including the UK, the United States and Australia. Each case study focuses on why they started a TTRPG club, what benefits they have seen from the club, what advice they'd give to other librarians hoping to start one and what they presented to leadership or management in order to get the club off the ground.

Case study 1: The Adventurers' Club
Rebecca String, Public Librarian at the Naperville Public Library in Naperville, Illinois, and Vice-President of the Games and Gaming Round Table of the American Library Association

Why did you start a TTRPG club?
We started at the Naperville Library in 2018 and wanted to start a TTRPG programme from the outset as we'd had requests from patrons to start a club. It took some work to get the Adventurers' Club off the ground.

What are the benefits of running the programme?
The kids have become friends through the group and have really come into themselves. It's a huge confidence builder. The librarians get to know the students and their characters, and they choose games that they know the kids will love. They select specific puzzles or storylines to help build a better programme.

For the kids to be able to interact with their friends, and seeing them blossom, has been very beneficial. To see a kid who doesn't contribute or is shy at first grow in confidence and show their creativity more and more as they visit the Club has been great to witness. We have received e-mails from the kids' parents telling us how much they love the Club and what it means to them.

The Club works well for the library's planning and we have different players coming to the library all the time.

What advice would you give to others hoping to run the programme?
Larger games like D&D are too huge for this kind of set-up, so we run games like No Thank You, Evil!, Magical Kitties Save the Day, My Little Pony: Tails of Equestria and other one-page RPGS like Tiniest Wizard, Definitely Wizards.

We look for indie games where we can print off a single-page rule sheet. It doesn't require boxes and boxes of material, it's simply a one-page sheet of rules. In my experience, the kids are excited to take the sheets home so they can play with their friends and family, including with their younger siblings.

To be able to read through the game quickly and to generate a new game at a rapid pace reduces the stress a great deal. When we explored the different types of TTRPGs with the students, we found that the players loved the variety and really enjoyed playing many different games. We also curate the kinds of games that appeal to those students who like science fiction TTRPGs, or to those who like high fantasy. We have a lot of kids who want to explore and build stories rather than engage in straight-up combat.

Anyone looking to get experience playing TTRPGs should join the Game Round Table RPG Guild. Be flexible and don't get stuck on the 'big' TTRPGs like D&D, because there are many alternatives out there. Pre-generated stories help with planning, but if you have to deviate that is fine because it's all about improvising. Don't be afraid to modify rules if it helps the group you are playing with. You are in charge. Make sure you set up expectations with the group you are running. Have a Session Zero [see Chapter 4]. Be kind and have fun!

My favourite TTRPGs that you can play over and over are No Thank You, Evil! and Amazing Tales. [These are both reviewed in Chapter 5.]

How is the programme delivered?
The Adventurers' Club started during the pandemic and we used Zoom because it was the platform which the schools in the area were using. Most of the programme was done in the Theatre of the Mind (ToTM) style. We would share our screen to show maps or monsters or other important events, but a lot of it was done as a ToTM. The team used a separate camera set-up facing a dice tray. The kids could roll at home and tell the GM their dice rolls, but those who did not have dice at home allowed the GM to roll and the kids could see their rolls over the camera – which is a really cool idea!

The kids that we worked with were eager to play in person from the beginning, and in my opinion it has helped with their socialisation to play in person. I and my colleagues will sometimes dress up as the theme and the kids are also encouraged to dress up as the monthly theme.

The Club is for Grades 3–6 (ages 8 to 12). Each programme runs for an hour and a half. It's hard to ensure that we get the same players for every single session. Because of this, we rely on 'one-shots' every session, which means the librarians and players have to get through the rules as fast as we can, which includes character creation, game play and a debrief within an hour and half. Also, we avoid long campaigns in general so that players don't miss out.

Registration is limited to six kids per game – any more than six, and the games become somewhat unruly. We haven't opened up the Adventurers' Club yet for teens to be GM, but this is something we are considering because the waiting list is getting so long.

The Naperville library system is very busy so we don't have to do a great deal of promotion. The monthly sign-ups for the TTRPG games are so popular that there are waiting lists for them.

How did you pitch the idea to the senior leadership team?
I and my colleagues submitted a proposal (see below, 'Kids' RPG club programme proposal') to the senior management team to get permission.

Case study 2: A TTRPG after-school club
Callum Stoner, Head of Mathematics and House System at Pitsford School, Northamptonshire, UK

Why did you start a TTRPG club?
As teachers at a private school, we are expected to offer three after-school activities between the hours of 4.20 and 5.20 after lessons have finished. The choice of activities is totally down to the teacher, and staff are encouraged to share their hobbies with the pupils. The History teacher runs an archaeology club, the Religious Studies teacher used to run an amateur radio club. My hobby has been role-playing since I was nine (and I'm now 47), so I decided to run a club after school. It has been running since I joined the school in 2003 and we have now had a group running continuously for the past 19 years. (Not always running D&D, sometimes dipping into Cthulhu, or Werewolf, but D&D is run for at least one term a year). Currently I have two groups running (Senior group formed of Years 9, 10 and 11 [ages 13 to 16] and Junior group formed of Years 7 and 8 [ages 11 to 13]).

What are the benefits of running the programme?
As part of the House Competition, there are regular debates that pupils are invited to take part in. Being part of the D&D group has allowed pupils who may have been introverted out of their shell a little. Some pupils have come out so much that they are taking school assemblies (not on D&D!) because they are now more confident in talking to their peers. I feel this is because they are allowed to talk about their opinions and not get drowned out by the more boisterous, loud pupils. Pupils with special educational needs, who have been school-phobic and don't enjoy lessons, really enjoy coming to the club, as it is an escape from reality, where they can play someone who doesn't have the same boundaries as them. I usually take the DM role, but occasionally a brave soul will take it on and make their own adventure and run it for the others. As a maths teacher, I find that it helps their mental arithmetic too.

What advice would you give to others hoping to run the programme?
Although I enjoy this part the best, character generation can be slow at the beginning, so it may be worth having some pre-generated characters ready to dive into a story with. D&D Beyond offers a free tool for creating and storing characters, so you could set a 'homework' where players make an account and build up a character for themselves. Don't make the group too big – six characters is more than enough. Don't let the loudest person dominate the group, and try to get the quietest person to be an integral part of any quests.

How is the programme delivered?
I run the groups after school. Junior (11-, 12- and 13-year-olds) is on Tuesday 4.20–5.20pm; Senior (14-, 15- and 16-year-olds) is on Monday at the same time.

How did you pitch the idea to the senior leadership team?
I never pitched it to my senior leadership team, although the first system I ran had both the Head and Deputy Head's daughters in. Quite a baptism by fire.

Case study 3: A student-initiated club
Kateri Wilson-Whalley, School Librarian, James Young High School, Livingston, Scotland

Why did you start a TTRPG club?
The pupils asked for it. Back in 2017 a group of senior pupils asked if I was willing to host a D&D group. To me, D&D was a level of geekery beyond where I was, but, never one to hold a pupil back on a scheme, I agreed to join the party. They helped me make a character, one of the pupils took on the DM role and we played every week after school for a couple of hours.

When they left there was only me and one other from that group but we decided we should run a club. We advertised and, lo and behold, there were around 12 pupils keen to play – which meant we needed at least two DMs. So I stepped up and took on the role. I got a senior pupil to meet weekly and coach me in various aspects of the game and help me to come up with solutions to the problems I'd created in my narrative. (They counted it as school volunteering.) Since then, there has continued to be a steady stream of pupils and every year I have to recruit some new DMs – I've had teachers, pupils and myself all running games.

What are the benefits of running the programme?
I really enjoy it. It turns out that making up fantasy stories and having a laugh with pupils is really enjoyable. It has given pupils a lot of benefits as well. In particular, a number of my autistic pupils have thrived – some even becoming confident DMs. It's helped their social interaction skills and their confidence, as they often are among the few at the table who have read the handbook and so they become an invaluable help to the DM and help to make the game run. As a result, their peers will defer to them and ask for help and advice when creating characters (depending on how much they know, the staff often defer to them as well).

I've also found for LGBTQ+ or shy pupils that it's a chance to role-play someone else – often an alternate gender or a more flamboyant character than they are in real life. Often these pupils hide in class, but in D&D they flourish, thanks to the creative and open nature of the world.

It's great for creating new friendships. I've got a number of pupils who have found good friends among their party and discovered communal love. I have even met other staff who love the game and I even play socially with one of them now out of school. It gives good pupils a chance to do slightly wilder things as well. The number of lovely pupils who turn into crazed pyromaniacs when given the ability to make fire is truly hilarious!

What advice would you give to others hoping to run the programme?
Play a game yourself. Before I started playing it had seemed hard to understand, but by actually playing I was quickly able to get a good grip on the basics.

Check out other games – The Adventure Zone podcast, Critical Role on YouTube etc. – but don't worry if your game isn't like that – every game is different and what these can do is offer ideas and skills you could try out.

Catch the Detentions & Dragons podcast – it's brilliant and full of ideas and details pitched at running a game in class or after school. Often D&D how-tos talk about running an adult game where you play for X number of hours in one setting, but that's not what a school game is like.

As with anything with a plan, the pupils will derail you, and having some ideas for what to do can help. If they insist on setting fire to everything, make it rain or take them onto water or have the clothing made of a magically fireproof substance. If they are ganging up on one pupil, have some magical pixies come and attack everyone but that person – perhaps they will prey on bullies and lurk, waiting for anyone being mean to somebody.

You will need a bit of prep time before the game so that you aren't floundering as DM, so just add a bit of extra time to your planning to accommodate that. As you gain experience the better you get at winging it and the less prep time you need (you might still want to do some prep, so that you can do awesome stuff, but you can do less if necessary).

There are lots of free or pay-what-you-want adventures available. They can be great as a starting point, or for pulling out bits simply for the adventure if the official books are a bit expensive to buy (I suggest that you buy a DM handbook, player handbook and monster manual at the very least). I've found that www.drivethrurpg.com has become a key source for me.

You don't need miniatures and maps, but a visual representation can be helpful. If you are on a tight budget a map doodled on paper and some paper figures (card folded in half vertically) can see you through. Other options include the pupils making their own Lego mini figures or using Warhammer or D&D miniatures. You can also create them virtually if tech is your thing, but I find that paper and pen is usually my default.

How is the programme delivered?
We play for an hour after school once a week, although if a group really wants to play more I can help to accommodate another lunchtime/after-school session. This year I have around 20 pupils playing weekly over three games. Pupils from S1 to S6 (ages 12 to 18) play. During the lockdowns we played virtually, either on a call or text based. We also do a day event, as part of which we play a game. This has varied over the years, but here are some examples.

Fantasy Con: We ran an hour-and-a-half pirate one-shot. Around 70 pupils attended the event, so we divided everyone into teams. I sourced DMs and wrote a game for it. We ran a session beforehand where we all created our characters, everyone got a D20 as part of the event and then divided into groups. A fair few of the DMs were new, and as a result we did the game in a way that could be easily worked through. (We ran through it prior to the event with the DMs.)

Space Con: This was a sci-fi based adventure. Eight teams of adventurers were given two hours to save a McGuffin in a spaceport. There was a map and each door/corridor had a number. As they opened a door they opened that number envelope and dealt with whatever they found. D20 were given as goodies, a DM was allocated to each table (though again not all had DM'd before, so it was all laid out for them) and characters were created in a quick-build session beforehand.

Comic Con: This was played virtually via TEAMS, divided into rooms. Each room played a Super-hero-themed adventure similar to the Fantasy Con game. Players had to make it through a Central Park-style setting and fight the big bad. We did a mix of text-based/video options depending on what people wanted, and both worked.

NB: For these, the characters are true D&D characters, but I used the Amazing Adventures character sheet option where there are a name, role and four things you are good at and therefore get a bonus on dice rolls. To make it even easier I preset the roles relevant to the adventure and allocated two things they were good at to each role.

How did you pitch the idea to the senior leadership team?
I didn't need to pitch it, I just did it. I argued for the first Comic Con event I ran (my annual day event), but once I had approval for that I've never had to do more than ask to run the event.

Case study 4: Introducing gaming into a learning resource centre
Patricia Snake, Hollingworth Academy, UK

Why did you start a TTRPG club?
As a long-time TTRPG lover, I love sharing my passions with my pupils, and from reading aloud many *Choose Your Own Adventure* stories to my classes in library lessons, I knew that many pupils would have a lot of fun playing. As our learning resource centre is often used for studying, I wanted to introduce a gamified/social aspect into the space, while also allowing pupils to develop key skills such as communication, problem solving and creative thinking.

What are the benefits of running the programme?
Since starting the club, I have seen many more previously unfamiliar faces in the library, as they now see it as a space for fun as well as study. We've had a huge buzz of excitement from staff and pupils, with children coming up to me all week initiating conversations about it. Pupils with educational learning plans are particularly enthusiastic. Many autistic pupils are seeing their special interest represented for the first time, and I'm delighted to give them a space to thrive. It also gives different year groups a chance to mix and unite over common interests when they might not have met otherwise.

What advice would you give to others hoping to run the programme?
I would definitely suggest buying the D&D Essentials Kit, as this comes with condensed rule books and pre-made characters as well as dice and a campaign – it's easy to get swept up in everything when you go down the rabbit hole, so having everything together in one pack made it much more manageable to get started. I would also suggest watching videos of people playing – to give you a feel of what role playing is and the responsibilities of a DM (don't forget, you're playing the game too, not just running it!).

Promote the club as much as you can – social media, posters around school, newsletters, assemblies, word of mouth. This goes for teachers too, because the more something is discussed, the more you will reach the people you want to!

Do an online survey in advance. This gave pupils a chance to tell me if they'd rather play or spectate, if they had any experience and any friends they wanted to play with. This helped me to match them into groups more easily. It also gave pupils whom I am unfamiliar with a chance to state their pronouns and any triggers or anxieties they had.

I recommend establishing ground rules in the first session and going over them every time. I make it clear that while they can take the campaign where they want, they must be respectful and keep everything school appropriate. Also – snacks! When in doubt, ply them with a box of Celebrations!

How is the programme delivered?
We currently run three campaigns in our library, which all run weekly after school on Mondays (2.50–3.30pm). We have a Learning Support Assistant, a librarian (me!) and an English teacher/member of the senior leadership team who all run their own campaign of about eight pupils each. All ages and genders attend, but primarily boys in Years 7–9 (ages 11 to 14) are present. The aim is to get pupils to DM when we have been running for longer. We also have a group who spectate.

How did you pitch the idea to the senior leadership team?
We didn't need to pitch the club to the senior leadership team. However, in our original discussions we emphasised both boosting the profile of the library and giving students a space to develop co-operation and communication skills. It helps that our English department is fully on board with the idea, so talking to like-minded teachers about the plan is a must!

Case study 5: D&D in Middle School (Years 6–8, ages 12–14)
Marie Gretch, Scotch College, Perth, Western Australia

Why did you start a TTRPG club?
The library runs a variety of clubs, and we try to change it each year so that we are 'branded' with particular clubs. Currently we run a Creative Writing Club, Book Club, Warhammer Club and eSports Club. We have previously run Coding Club, Maker Space, Chess Club and Anime Film Club. Other middle school (MS) teachers run Board Games, Lego Club, Robotics Club, Cooking for the Homeless Club, Community Service Club, as well as clubs for students who enter academically oriented state and national competitions (Da Vinci, Philosothon). We also aim to run clubs that are not academically or socially elitist, that all years can join, that cost the students nothing and are just about having fun and, most importantly, making connections with other 'like interested' students. We have a large, flexible MS library space that allows lots of different things to happen at the same time at lunchtime, and we have the staff to supervise the club, so it is all an easy fit.

What are the benefits of running the programme?
The benefits for the library are that it is a cool, fun club that we are associated with. It softens the traditional role of the library a little and broadens our role and how students see us. It allows opportunities for library staff to have conversations with students whom they might not normally interact with outside of class. There is an activity at lunchtime that students can do when there are no other activities that suit their interest. It provides a place and space for a student to 'join in' without necessarily being locked into or aligned with any particular group of students.

It is a free, fun, maintenance-free activity for students to participate in. It provides opportunities for students to meet like-minded students that they usually wouldn't mix with and thus provides opportunities for connections to be made and friendships formed.

What advice would you give to other librarians hoping to run the programme?
Some students become too bossy and this needs to be explained to that student early on. We have a no exclusion policy – we don't boss others around, exclude anyone from the action/plot lines or have racist plot lines or stereotypically racist creatures etc. We give a ten-minute time warning to the group to wind up the action and storyline for the week and help pack up. D&D has had some historical bad publicity and this needs to be properly addressed early on with parents if an issue is raised. We need to ensure that all understand this is storytelling role-play in person, not gaming.

Some students with a lot of resources bring boards, figures, models etc. This is allowed if they can be freely used and shared among the group. Our emphasis is on playing without any special resources, just hand-made maps and dice.

How is the programme delivered?
D&D Club operates as a co-curricular club. Co-curricular clubs are generally run during lunchtimes or after school. Most are vertical across years, so Year 6, 7 and 8 (ages 11 to 14) all join in the same club. An e-mail goes out in Week 1 of each of the four terms and boys nominate for whatever and how many clubs they want to join and just show up. If it is a lunchtime club, boys bring their lunch and drink and have it during the club.

Students cannot form their own groups. Groups are organised by the teachers on the first day, and a mix of able and experienced players, beginners and boys who have never played before are allocated to each group. But there is a lot of conciliation and collaborative decision making about groups, so all are happy. Students attend D&D Club once a week. It is explained that boys must attend every week, otherwise other students and the game (campaign) are affected. Students play one game (campaign) for the whole term, which is usually about nine to ten weeks.

Boys come with their lunches to the library in the space set aside for the club. The club has become so big that Year 6 have their club on Friday lunchtimes for a 40-minute campaign; at present there are six groups playing concurrently in the same space. Year 7 and 8 have their club on Wednesday for 40 minutes; at present there are eight groups running concurrently.

Students may bring their own resources, but initially the library purchased sets of D&D dice online, one set for each group. We also provided paper and pens for anyone who liked to draw their own maps. We purchased a couple of the physical D&D books – the Starters' Set and Players' Handbook, and later a Monster Manual. But there are also copies of all resources available online. All equipment is left in the room in a cupboard.

The first week, groups are worked out and a DM is allocated. If a group has no experienced DM, then a staff member takes that role until a student feels they can take it on. Staff will run sessions for DMs 'in waiting' if needed.

How did you pitch the idea to the senior leadership team?
Generally, co-curricular clubs are offered for their academic merit, but a submission was made by the MS staff that clubs needed to offer comradeship and companionship – a place where boys could find students with common interests

across the campus. The pitch was aimed at the well-being of boys from a holistic viewpoint. Although D&D does attract more academically talented students, it can be played by the whole range of students, regardless of academic, social, emotional or economic status. Students with special needs, inclusivity and diversity points of difference, or from financially challenged homes can all play. D&D has processes and procedures that maths players love, that artistic and creative students love, that storytellers love and those bossy students can love! It also has a place for quiet students who like to watch others and feel comfortable first before launching into a game. All these qualities were good selling points to encourage the school leaders to allow this club to happen. This is a club that can run with minimal expenditure – you just need a set of dice per group.

Kids' RPG club programme proposal

The following is a sample TTRPG gaming proposal kindly provided by Rebecca Strang, Public Librarian in Naperville, Illinois. Using this proposal, Rebecca was able to secure funding for a very popular TTPRG gaming programme.

Proposal for children's role-playing game club
Name or theme of programme: Adventurers' Club
Age targeted by programme: Ages 8–12 years
Length and frequency of programmes: 1.5 hrs once per month
Registration required or not: Yes, limit 12 (6 children per game master)
Number of staff to implement the programme at each building: 2

Event description: Learn how to play storytelling board games, role-playing games and more. Go on adventures to rescue unicorns, pretend to be a magical animal, discover what stuffed animals are up to when you're asleep! Limited to 12 participants in 3rd to 6th grade [ages 8 to 12].

Session example: 20 minutes to explain the setting/rules; 50 minutes to play/create; 10 minutes to recap and share favourite moments; 10 minutes for buffer. Provide pre-generated characters (when necessary) to eliminate the time it takes to create a character (though it would be great to have a separate programme that could serve as an intro to RPGs, maybe an information session for parents and children and some time to create a character). We can also include things like having children share written work or art related to the stories we create. (Easily done online or in person with limited unshared supplies.)

RPGs are more than D&D, there are also several RPG systems developed specifically with children in mind, as well as other oral storytelling games, card games and board games. An ongoing programme could explore several of these. These games offer many benefits in addition to being TONS OF FUN, such as helping children to practise socialisation and communication skills, teamwork, problem solving, creative thinking and storytelling. Participating in these games can help to boost confidence and empathy and usually requires reading and often maths. It's a creative STEAM [science, technology, engineering, art and maths] activity that has benefits that last beyond the time spent playing at the table.

Supplies required:
- Game rules and character sheets
- RPG dice (at least 14 sets; one set per player and game guide)
- Pencils (at least 14; one per player and game guide)
- Clipboards (14; one per player and game guide – some games will involve movement, so a portable writing surface will be useful)
- Coloured pencils/crayons (for some RPGs that have colourable character sheets)

RPG examples:
- Amazing Tales – 'The best stories are the ones you make up with your children. That's the thought behind Amazing Tales, a story making game of roleplay and imagination for children who are old enough to have adventures. With the very simple Amazing Tales rules as a guide, you and your child can make up stories together, rolling dice to add drama and excitement for everyone.' https://amazing-tales.net
- Cloud Dungeon / Sunken Dungeon / ExSpelled – 'It's designed to be parent+kid friendly. It has permanent consequences and interesting group decisions to make, but is forgiving. It's easy to get into. It's all about making unique characters, coloring/drawing, and customizing. It's an incredibly fun and creative experience that appeals to anyone who likes to make stuff.' www.andhegames.com
- Hero Kids – A fantasy RPG designed for players aged 4–10. Rules are simple and adventures are designed specifically for the age group it was designed for. Available through Drive-Thru RPG. herokidsrpg.blogspot.com
- Kids on Bikes / Kids on Brooms – 'Kids on Bikes is a Collaborative Storytelling RPG set in small towns with big adventure! In Kids on Bikes, you take on the roles of everyday people grappling with strange, terrifying, and very, very powerful forces that they cannot defeat, control, or even fully understand. Kids on Bikes even allows you to create a communally controlled Powered Character to add another dimension of gameplay to your games!' https://renegadegamestudios.com/kids-on-bikes
- Magical Kitties Save the Day – 'You are magical kitties. You have humans. The humans have problems. Use your magical powers to solve their problems and save the day! A role-playing game designed for all ages to enjoy, that excels as an introduction to the hobby. The elegantly simple rules system puts the emphasis on storytelling and supports a setting and characters that players are familiar with and love from the start.' www.atlas-games.com/magicalkitties
- My Little Pony: Tails of Equestria – 'Tails of Equestria allows you to create, name and play as your very own pony character to solve puzzles and explore dungeons, there may even be some dragons! . . . Tails of Equestria is not about getting to the end of a board or having the most points but about having fantastical adventures along the way and using the magic of friendship to overcome any obstacles that stand in your way. As a group. You and your friends, including the GM, are all on the same team – as long as every pony

is having fun, everybody wins!' https://riverhorse.eu/our-games/my-little-pony-tails-of-equestria

- No Thank You, Evil! – 'Great fun for kids as young as five years old. But it's also great fun for the rest of family – adults included! – because the scalable rules adapt easily to the abilities of the player. After a game or two with the grown-ups, a twelve-year-old might even run games for the other kids! The gameplay rules are easy to grasp for novice or young players, but nuanced and flexible enough for older kids and grown-ups to enjoy just as much.' www.nothankyouevil.com
- Stuffed Fables – A hybrid RPG-board game 'in which players take on the roles of brave stuffies seeking to save the child they love from a scheming, evil mastermind. Make daring melee attacks, leap across conveyor belts, or even steer a racing wagon down a peril-filled hill. The game delivers a thrilling narrative driven by player choices. Players explore a world of wonder and danger, unlocking curious discoveries. The chapters of Stuffed Fables explore the many milestones of a child's life, creating a memorable tale ideal for families, as well as groups of adults who haven't forgotten their childlike sense of wonder.' https://boardgamegeek.com/boardgame/233312/stuffed-fables
- Tiniest Wizard – 'You are a tiny wizard, as small as a drawing on a business card. You do magic in the form of single-word spells taken from a dictionary. At a tiny scale, even a house offers ample opportunity for adventure. On your adventures will you encounter big bugs, tiny dragons, ancient room guardians, or something only you can imagine?' https://mitchelldaily.itch.io/tiniest-wizard
- Tiny Dungeon 2E – 'With streamlined mechanics that utilize only one to three single six-sided dice on every action, characters that can be written 3x5 notecard, and easy to understand and teach rules, Tiny Dungeon 2e is great for all groups, ages and experience levels!' www.gallantknightgames.com/tiny-dungeon-2e
- WanderSquares – A hybrid RPG-board game where you can 'Join the Wanderkind, a secret order of adventurers who roam the known worlds seeking mysteries and fighting for justice. You can choose from four classes and four kinds: play as a brave knight, a powerful wizard, a clever trickster or a quick-footed scout. Your first mission takes place on the forest world of Undwen, in the Winding Wood.' www.wandersquares.com

3 How Do I Start and What Do I Need?

What you will need

Before I launch into how to start a TTRPG in your library, I will first provide some information on what you need to have at the ready in order to play a TTRPG. In reality, the items you need to run a TTRPG can be as complex or as simple as you like. You will need to adapt it to the needs of your players and the budget you have access to.

In my opinion all you need to get started are tables, enough to sit six people around comfortably (Figure 3.1); scrap paper; pencils (not pens); and of course dice (Figure 3.2 on the next page). In Chapter 5 there is a list of 20 TTRPGs other than D&D that you can play in your library, with short reviews and a synopsis of each game.

Figure 3.1 *Table and chairs set out for game playing*

Most, if not all, TTRPGs require some sort of dice system to play; however, many require only standard six-sided dice which can be easily sourced. The other kind of dice, which range from four-sided up to 20-sided, can be purchased in sets for approximately £7.00 (USD 8.00).

All in all, dice should not cost you a lot. Once students become interested in TTRPGs, they will often come with their own dice. In my

Figure 3.2 *Different types of dice*

library I have found that students have a personal connection with their dice and, like many adults who play TTRPGs, consider some dice lucky or unlucky. One student in our school who plays in the library regularly builds his own dice jail where other players like to place their own unlucky dice that appear to be rolling consistently low numbers!

I also suggest getting a binder with clear plastic sheets. This will be a lifesaver when it comes to storing information like campaign storylines and copies of players' character sheets. I also use binders to hold upcoming fights, so if I know players will most likely be encountering a monster, I print off all of its statistics, mannerisms and abilities and have it ready to go in the binder. The same goes for magical or important items that I think the students might come across, as well as NPCs. I discuss player backstories and more in Chapter 4.

I would encourage players, especially in a school setting, to have a folder or binder because it can be stressful for them if they misplace their character sheets or other important information. Our players typically use soft-back journals where they stick their sheets in so they don't lose them. They can then write down any additional items they might pick up or any important notes in the journal.

It is not required to have this next item, but I also enjoy using a three-legged whiteboard that comes with flipchart paper. I do this for a few reasons. I sometimes prop it up next to the table where we are playing to draw a quick map of where the players are (Figure 3.3 opposite), or I might write out a riddle or puzzle that they may need to spend some time on. The flip chart is also valuable when it comes to the order of players in a combat situation. Having this kind of visual is very helpful for me as a GM and for the players. You could also use it to remind players of rules or

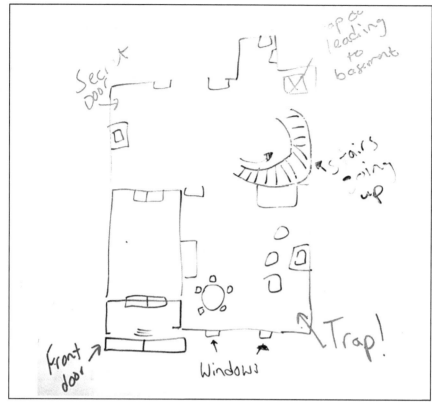

Figure 3.3 *Game map drawn on a whiteboard*

upcoming games, especially if you are in a public library setting where you don't see the players on a daily basis.

Initiative tracker

What's an initiative tracker? It's simply a way for you keep track of whose turn it is when combat erupts. It's an important part of TTRPGs because combat is meant to be fast and exciting, and if you forget whose turn it is or you aren't organised, it can slow everything down. In reality, all you really need to keep track of initiative is scrap paper. However, there are multiple kinds of initiative trackers available that might be of use. These trackers often have tables for hit points, Armour Class and other stats for you to keep track of (Figure 3.4 on the next page). I also use them for nostalgia purposes. I like to flip through the trackers and see the dates when our students had important battles and encounters. I write notes in the margins regarding any funny or interesting moments they've had. These can also

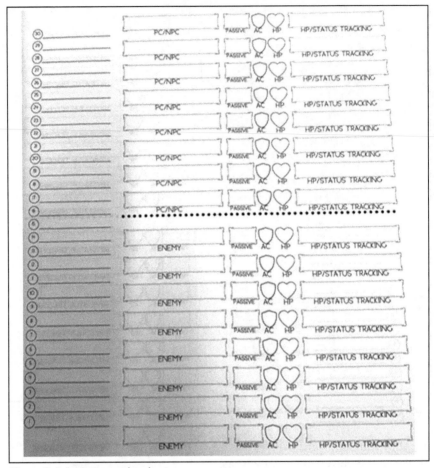

Figure 3.4 *Initiative tracker sheet*

save time when it comes to finding somewhere to write down initiative. Having a book handy with everything in one place can be very useful. There are even online initiative trackers if you are using a computer, laptop or tablet and find this easier. One of my favourites is from DM Tools and can be found here: https://dm.tools/tracker.

Whatever you decide to use, my advice is to ensure that your players can see the turn order. This will save time and confusion and keep everyone at the ready. It's also a good idea to remind players when they are next - it lets them prepare for what they want to do and this in turn will save time. Another quick method is to simply fold a revision or recipe card over the top of your GM screen (if you are using one) with the characters' names running right to left (from your perspective) so the players in front of you can see what the order is.

Maps

In the library setting, you don't really need maps. Time will be short and you and the players should probably rely on ToTM, where you all imagine what's going on. That said, I occasionally use maps when I want to bring to life an important battle. Luckily, several kinds of dry-erase grid maps are available with interlocking pieces that can make map making a lot of fun and not take a ton of time. There are also pre-made maps that you can adapt to your adventure. These are usually dry erase, so you can add notes or other elements to them. If you are interested in dry-erase maps, a great one is available from Melee Mats in the USA.[1] If you are short on time and budget however, I recommend using flip chart paper or scrap paper.

Even better, ask your players if one of them wants to be the designated map maker, especially if they find themselves in a dungeon. Give the players some graph paper and let them draw their own, just like their characters would have to if they were trying to figure out where they were going. Maps can make the experience more involved.

Virtual TTRPG platforms

There is a wide variety of online formats you can use if you think playing online is more attuned to your situation. Just like the in-person game, virtual playing can be as in-depth or as basic as you like.

When we went into lockdown in 2020, I had just started a TTRPG campaign with a group of amazing 13-year-old students. They were immediately asking about playing online, so I sent a letter home to their parents explaining the game, how much fun it is to play and how the students and I benefit from it.

My school was already using Microsoft Teams to conduct online lessons and I was also using this format to deliver daily library lessons. Using MS Teams, and with parental permission, I ran near-daily TTRPG sessions during lunchtime and sometimes after school and even during the Christmas holidays.

The set-up was very simple: I created a 'lesson' and the students logged into MS Teams the same way as for a regular class or lesson. None of us turned our cameras on; rather, I relied on voice communication from them and what I did was share my screen, placing various pictures, drawings and images on the screen for them to look at while we played. It worked very well, and in my opinion using this ToTM method can sometimes be more effective than getting involved with expensive maps, mini figures or other items.

It was very beneficial to run the programme virtually because it meant that when we were allowed back in person, the students hadn't missed a beat of their campaign, or their characters or the game itself. It also kept them connected to the library in a very unique way. In Chapter 1 I discussed selling the game to the powers that be. Keeping track of player engagement is also a way to ensure that management understands how important this game is to the students, and can help with future requests for budget, time and space.

Running an online TTRPG session

There are positives and negatives to running a TTRPG session online. The games, by design, are meant to be played in person. In my experience this is how you get the most out of the game, by being with your friends in this shared experience. Put that shared experience in a safe, inclusive space like a library, and you have a recipe for success.

However, there are benefits to running a TTRPG online. In my experience, younger players get much less distracted, or, if they are pulled away from the game, they can mute themselves. In real life, if a player gets bored or distracted it can sometimes have a knock-on effect and derail the game. Playing online is extremely helpful to any student who might be feeling anxious about playing in person. In a virtual setting they do not have to show their face, they can mute themselves if they want to and they can engage when it's their turn or when they feel comfortable. I feel that playing online for so long during lockdown really gave several of our students a lot of confidence and helped them play in person when we returned to school.

Online playing means that a player's focus is often 100% on the game, making it run more smoothly. It also means that you can play for longer, because there is little to no set-up for an online game other than turning your device on. Rolling can all be done on screen, or let the students roll at home and tell you their rolls (you may get a lot of natural 20s this way!).

Roll20

I think Roll20 is one of the most popular virtual TTRPG systems; at least, it's the one I hear about the most and the one I use for my personal TTRPG sessions that are non-library related. As GM, you will have a screen in front of you displaying a map or image. You get to choose what the players can or cannot see. For example, you have a map of a forest with a road going through the middle. You upload this to Roll20, right click on it and add it to the Map Layer. Every player who logs in can see the map. The players then upload their characters' images and add them to the Token Layer; they can be images they drew themselves or ones they've purchased elsewhere. The players drag the images onto the map and can move them around at will.

However, you have three goblins hiding in the woods that you want to jump out and attack the players. You upload the goblins to the map but you add them to the GM Layer, meaning that only you can see them. When the time is right, you move them to the side of the road, right click on them and add them to the Token Layer, which means the players can now be surprised that three creatures just leapt out of the woods at them.

The dice rolling is all done within Roll20's mechanics: it can be done by clicking a button that represents the dice you want to roll or by actually typing in the roll command in the chat screen. For example, if you wanted to roll a six-sided dice you would type in /r 1d6; if you wanted to roll two six-sided dice at once, you'd type in /r 2d6, and so on.

The basic system is free to play; however, to sign up you need an e-mail address and unique username for each student. This might not be something the students' parents are keen on, so ensure that you have all proper permissions in place before you use a system like Roll20. Also, as much as I do like it, there is something of a learning curve with Roll20, so I really recommend that you become familiar with it yourself before unleashing it on the students, who might find it as overwhelming as I did when I first started.

Zoom

I have spoken to a lot of librarians who have used Zoom, not MS Teams, to deliver online TTRPG sessions and there are many similarities with what works and what doesn't. One thing that stands out, and this would apply to Roll20 as well, is that a lot can be lost in playing online TTRPGs. This is because the game itself is only one piece of the puzzle. There is a lot to be said for the tension, the excitement, the drama that comes only with being in person. This can be applied to watching a movie on a laptop as opposed to seeing it in the cinema or seeing a live production. The camaraderie and atmosphere that are generated during an in-person game are nearly impossible to replicate online. However, if playing online works for your players and their situations, don't let me discourage you. As I've already mentioned, we played online for a long time and it was a lifesaver for me, and I feel that it greatly benefited the students.

On Zoom, as in person, it's important that players all take turns and not talk over each other. Using the turn system discussed in Chapter 4 works just as well online. My advice on Zoom is to use it as an audio function, but also use Roll20 for the visual. However, if you want to completely use ToTM, you can find some great ambient music on YouTube that is royalty free and is TTPRG based. This involves using music when players are in combat, are exploring different settings or are strolling through the town. Pulling up my YouTube search history will find several instances of 'RPG Tavern Brawl Sound'. Whatever setting you are in, I recommend doing this, as the feedback I've had from adult players is that they absolutely love being sent this music.

How to start your TTRPG programme

If you're wondering how to start a TTRPG in your library, the best advice is to jump straight in. I know that's easier said than done, but it really is the best thing to do. It's easy to feel overwhelmed, but you can really get started easily and quickly by bringing in a few players and starting small. From my perspective, I saw the desire on the part of the students and have had the core group of students take part twice weekly in the library for over three years now; they have not missed a session and are always eager to play. We even have our own students running sessions for younger students, which has a ton of social and emotional benefits for everyone involved. A great aspect of this TTRPG programme is that students of many different ages have bonded and become friends. I feel this is very unique in schools. We have players who are 11 years old sitting at tables with 16-year-olds talking about the games, reading the books, sharing jokes and stories and simply hanging out in between sessions. You don't see this in other settings, and I know from anecdotal evidence that these students from widely different backgrounds and situations are hanging out after school, playing TTRPGs on the weekends and forming strong friendships.

Starting a TTRPG in your library can be very easy, if using pre-made campaigns. If you have endless time and want to make your own adventure, that is amazing and I will be eternally jealous of you. However, if, like many people, you do not have a lot of time on your hands, then a pre-made adventure is essential. Again, in Chapter 5 there is a list of 20 TTRPGs that can be easily plugged into your library setting. If you are going down the D&D route, that is also amazing, and I strongly recommend that you purchase the Starter Set. This is affordable and comes with pre-made character sheets, an amazing adventure and a condensed version of the Player's Handbook. It contains everything you need to get your players from level one to five and it's a lot of fun. If you are thinking about D&D in your library and are feeling overwhelmed, the Starter Set will remove this anxiety, as it's a one-stop shop for everything you need.

Again, all of this depends on your budget. You can purchase pre-made campaigns at bookshops which can cost upwards of £30 each. Or you can visit a site called DM Guild or Drive-Thru RPG: they both have a huge array of approved TTRPG adventures for a much lower price. In fact, some of the adventures that are considered a 'one shot' (about four hours in length to play) are usually £1 or 'pay what you want'.

You've got the kit, an adventure, pencils and a notebook. Now you need players. You might find this isn't a problem at all, like I did; but I recommend, if you can, seeking out slightly older players. I started out with players who were aged 13; they are now 15 and some of them run their own sessions. For me, having 13-year-olds made it easier, as they were slightly more mature than the 11-year-olds and I found it easier to get started.

However, the best way to play is simply to dive and give it a try. If you are using a pre-made campaign I strongly suggest reading this through in its entirety before launching it. Even reading a few chapters ahead of the students will help you immensely. While reading, take notes – this will save you a ton of time and avoid a lot of confusion.

Getting the word out

You may feel that you don't need to bring any new faces to the table for your TTRPG programme. You may have students constantly asking you to start a TTRPG programme in your library, and that's why you are here. If that is the case, awesome – you can probably skip this chapter. Or, you can read through it and gather ideas for the future in case you do feel that you need to bring in new faces.

How did I start the programme? I, like millions of other people, became hooked on *Stranger Things*, which is very closely linked to D&D and has become even more intertwined as the series has progressed. When *Stranger Things* first aired, students were really buzzing about the show. They were constantly asking me if I'd seen it and I had to cover my ears so nothing would be spoiled. Students also began talking about D&D, and this rekindled my interest in it. At that time I hadn't played the game in quite a while, although I still read fantasy novels like *The Name of the Wind* by

Patrick Rothfuss, which is absolutely amazing, as well as the *Wheel of Time* series by Robert Jordan. I decided on the following course of action:

> On a whiteboard that students can interact with as they enter the library, I wrote, 'Should We Start a D&D Programme in the Library?' There were three columns: Yes / No / What is D&D?
>
> Within a day, a student had taken it upon themselves to write in the third column: 'The game from Stranger Things'. After that, the 'Yes' column was so filled with check marks that it became an indiscernible mess.
>
> I quickly made a sign-up sheet and it filled up within a few days.

If you feel this approach won't be enough, there are other ways. If you are in a school library you can ask to visit classrooms to advertise. Ask student librarians to make posters and spread the word. Whether you work in public or in school libraries, you will be aware of the students who are artistic and enjoy making posters. I have a 16-year-old TTRPG player in my school who loves to sketch posters and enhance them digitally.

If you do decide to make your own posters, I recommend using Canva. This is a free graphic design website that uses a simple drag-and-drop method that is very easy to use. You can also sign up as an educator and receive more perks and access to what already is a great programme. It can create an effective poster advertising your club in a very short period of time.

Strategies that I use to get the word out for library programmes, and ones that I will use if our TTRPG programme ever loses an audience, include the following:

Speaking at year-group assemblies. These are very effective, as you get to speak to a large group. Even more effective is speaking in front of an entire school, which I'm fortunate to do a few times a year. Our school has around 1,700 students, therefore if I'm promoting a programme in an assembly of this size, it usually fills up quickly. I also visit classrooms during students' registration or tutor time.

Surveys. You can also survey the students more formally. You might find that those who are eager to play will be happily surprised that you are hoping to run a TTRPG programme. Asking tweens and teens what they want is important to do from day one, and will help with any programme.

Speaking to other teachers. I speak out during staff briefing and put upcoming programmes in the weekly staff bulletin. You never know which TTRPG fans are lurking around in your school – they may also have ideas for students who would want to play. Keeping teachers or, if you work in the public library, school librarians informed of your TTPRG programme will be hugely beneficial. Adults who have regular contact with youth will be able to spread the word at a faster level.

Sending letters home to parents. I send letters explaining that the game will be launched on a specific date, what it is and the benefits of taking part. Communicating to parents in this way can also quell any anxiety they may have. We also send a newsletter home to parents, so information about TTRPG programmes can go in there too. It might not be an issue now, but in the past these types of games stirred up a lot of fear in religious sectors, which translated into problems for educators who were promoting them. The games listed in Chapter 5 have age ratings attached, which I hope will be useful. You will know the maturity level of your players and will be able to work out what games they should be playing.

Displays and posters. Creating displays works in both public and school libraries. A simple *Stranger Things* display with our D&D-style books (see Chapter 5 for a reading list) was very popular and helped to increase the interest in the game itself. Public libraries usually have a much stronger web presence than school libraries, as some have marketing departments. It may not be feasible for all, but if you have a good relationship with your marketing department you can possibly create a few high-quality posters or images for the library's website and for the areas you serve.

Visits to schools. When I worked in a public library, I would visit local high schools and ask permission to put up posters. I had a drop-in session in the school library (hopefully the schools near you have this) and asked the school librarians to spread the word. Doing this helped to establish a good relationship with the school librarians and resulted in us working together for many other projects. In my experience, teachers and staff in schools are usually more than happy for someone to come in and speak to the students. Not only does it make for a break in the routine, it allows you to spread the word about other events at the public library where you work. I also sent e-mails to teachers in the high schools.

Social media. If your school or public library allows social media and has a social media presence, these can be very valuable when it comes to advertising and promoting your TTRPG programme. I advertised on my public library's social media accounts and websites. This helped to establish a TTRPG culture in the library, which spread quickly via word of mouth. You may not be reaching the players themselves, but you might be successful in reaching their parents, which is the next best thing.

However you market your programme, it's a good idea to use imagery, and use as few words as possible. When using images, I recommend visiting the site Pixabay (https://pixabay.com) for royalty- and copyright-free images; you can find many TTRPG-related images on this site. As an example for text, one of our student posters reads, 'Dungeons & Dragons Club in the Library! Ask Mr. Maxwell For More Details!'. Behind these words are multi-sided dice and images of adventurers confronting a dragon in front of its lair. This poster is evergreen because there are no dates or times on it. We did this because you never know when the times of the programme may change. The information is clear and to the point. Students know that all they need to do if they have an interest in D&D is come to the library and ask me.

The above methods can be applied to almost any library programme. My advice is to be ruthless, persistent and aggressive in your advertising methods. This will bring new faces to your library to try these games out.

I also enjoy tying in books for the players to read in between gaming sessions. This is a great way to market the library and keep the players engaged in literature. There is a full reading list in Chapter 5.

What if too many students sign up? This is a good problem to have, but it's still a problem. There is a section in Chapter 4 on creating great GMs out of your teen players. I strongly recommend asking your teens to help if you think they have time and are interested in doing so. I have created a waiting list for those who are interested and have encouraged them to create characters and read TTRPG books in the library before and after school. I think setting up multiple sessions is a challenge, but worth doing if you can find the right teen GM.

In the public library setting, Strang (2022) states that her public library has a long waiting list of youth players. This is the reality of creating a popular programme, and it can be frustrating when you know you have people waiting to play.

Zero-preparation games

There is a lot to be said for running a TTRPG with zero preparation. Sure, it can be anxiety inducing, but, just like anything else, it gets a lot easier with time. Here are some tips for running a TTRPG with zero prep.

Choose wisely

In Chapter 5 I list 20 TTRPG alternatives to D&D. Many of these require little to no preparation. If you are in a school or public library and feel that you have almost no time to spare, choose your TTRPG wisely. You may find that larger-scope games like D&D or Pathfinder are simply too large to take on. In my interview with Illinois public librarian Rebecca Strang (2022), she stated that once she got her patrons playing No Thank You, Evil! and other games, they didn't even ask about the more famous games like D&D.

The issue here is that games like D&D and Pathfinder are famous: there are countless books, spinoffs and, of course, TV shows and films that revolve around them. Your library users are going to be aware of these names even if they haven't played them. Your role, if you want to try something else, is to simply steer them away by showing them how great the alternatives are. My opinion is that once they are hooked, they won't look back.

Let the players help

I had an 'a-ha!' moment once while playing D&D with teenagers in the library. I had done a ton of preparation as usual and had a big speech about the description of the location the students had wandered into. It wasn't vital to the overall plot but I thought they'd enjoy it. As I launched into the minutiae of the jungle plants and broken statues that they were seeing, one student tossed his pencil onto the table, leaned back and said, 'This is when Mr Maxwell talks for a while.'

'Do I do that a lot?'

'Yes!' came the collective response.

I realised that when I did this, it wasn't really their game, it was mine, and I should be handing it back to them. From then on I tried to give fewer speeches and more time for them to interact. When you're short on time, this will be essential.

Zero-preparation games mean you are all in it together. In many ways you are all in it together no matter what you play, but in a game where you have purposely done no prep your players need to be both aware of this and fully on board to help out. Let's face it, no one likes to play a game where one person stands up and delivers an eight-minute info dump on the history of the family-run stable you've just entered. Let the players tell the story about the tavern, inn, town or whatever scenario they are in. Let the players name the NPCs, the pets and even the villains if you want to. Trust me, this will make it much more fun and your players will be more engaged. Once they figure out that they are just as responsible for creating the story as you, they will start to do it without asking.

The challenge with letting the players help, especially younger players, is that the 'story' can devolve very quickly into Player versus Player (PvP) combat. This should be avoided at all costs, and the players can be reminded of the rules that PvP is not allowed unless it's part of the story. What do I mean by this? The following is a scenario where PvP happened in the campaign our students were in.

> The players entered a room, it was empty except for a throne made of bones. I knew that whoever sat on the throne had a chance of having their minds taken over by an evil demon. The players did not know this, nor did they bother to check to see if the chair was magic or had any other special qualities. One of the players simply walked over and decided to rest his weary feet by sitting on the throne.
>
> The player rolled very poorly against the chair's magic, and therefore had his mind taken over. In my notes I had written down that if that happened, the player was to attack the creature that was nearest to him. This turned out to be the group's wizard, who was easily taken down by the player had who sat in the chair.
>
> Nobody knew what was going on. It was very 'out of character' for the player to act in this way, and he role-played it very well at the table. Needless to say, the other players did pile onto him to stop him from doing further damage, and once he had taken a certain amount of damage and enough time had passed, the mind control was over and he was back to his normal, loveable self.

In this instance, the PvP fully served the story, the teens knew it was part of the overall doom and gloom they were used to in this particular dungeon and they easily moved on from it. If it's not part of the story, my experience is that real-life feelings can be hurt when players fight each other or pile on to each other, therefore it needs to be addressed from the start.

You do not need to create new worlds

I discuss this in Chapter 4 in more detail, but new GMs often panic and think that they need to create brand new worlds from scratch. You definitely do not need to do this. I've been running TTRPGs in my school library for three years and the moments that the students talk about time and time again are the ones where funny, weird and unexpected things happened. These are things that I could not have prepared for if you had given me 1,000 years of preparation time. Go with the flow, let the players drive the story.

You've got the ideas

Many new GMs who are thinking of running a TTRPG might feel that they simply don't have enough ideas in their head to run a session, let alone run one without preparing. This may be untrue. Camp (2020) asks new GMs to consider the fact that their minds are full of ideas from television, movies, books and perhaps board games. All you need to do is mix these ideas up and generate story ideas. These plot hooks and stories are all in your mind, you just need to access them in a way that serves your story.

So, how do you go about doing this, exactly? It's all about asking the right questions without overwhelming the players, says Camp (2020), and there are several ways to do this - but it's important that the questions match the world that your characters are building.

Camp (2020), provides some examples of the kinds of questions you can use:

Description questions: What does it look like?
Speculation questions: Why do you think that is? What could be the reason?
Lore questions: What do you know about this?
Action questions: What do you do?
Character questions: Who are you? What drives you?
Choice questions: What do you choose?

Using these questions in a balanced environment where you, as the GM, are also answering some of these questions will allow a co-operative play that gives you freedom to prepare nothing, or near to nothing, for each session.

As mentioned in Chapter 2, many librarians state that their players prefer ToTM as opposed to having access to large maps, figures and other visual props. I really love this idea of making TTRPG sessions more collaborative as opposed to having a GM dictating everything. Of course, the age group of the players must be taken into account, but in my experience of working with ages 11-16, these age groups can come up with very fun, ingenious and odd things that will make your session even more interesting and engaging.

The following is another example from Camp (2020) that asks the players to fill in the blanks.

GM: You are all dangling from a rope. What is it attached to?
Player 1: It's attached to an airship that is flying above a city.

In this short, simple example, the GM or players can then work out a few things: who owns the airship? Is it a cult that worships a dragon that lives in the mountains? Is it a band of adventurers who are seeking lost treasure? Is the airship powered by a living being like a fire elemental? What does the airship look like? Does it have any weapons attached to it? What is the name of the city? Maybe the airship belongs to the city and was stolen by someone and this has now implicated the adventurers.

Working together, you and the players can create a great adventure by asking the right questions and using the information that is already stored in your mind. I would highly recommend the entire 80-page *Prepless Game Master* by Paul Camp.[2]

Notes

1   https://meleemats.com/products/copy-of-distressed-dry-erase-grid-mat
2   *Prepless Game Master* can be purchased from: https://dungeonvault.com/the-prepless-gamemaster

4 Session Zero and Beyond

Beginning GM: relax, and breathe

Before I launch into Session Zero, what it is and how to run it, I will provide some tips for a beginning GM.

It can feel very overwhelming to be a GM for the first time - I definitely felt huge nerves. Even when starting it with younger audiences, it can be anxiety inducing. What if I mess up? What if I forget all the information? What if the players are bored?

My advice is to throw all of those questions out of the window because it doesn't matter. What matters is that you have fun, and if you forget something, so what? Look it up, or make something up and move on. I can't tell you how many times I've improvised on a rule just to keep the game moving, only to find out later I had made the wrong decision. The world didn't end. My main rule is that I will be fair to the players if I don't know a rule and can't find the answer quickly. If the question being asked involves the death of a character or they are trying to solve a really difficult puzzle, then yes, I will pause things to look up the ruling, but otherwise I try to keep things flowing as smoothly as possible. My main rule is that you should always let your players' characters try something as long as it isn't mean or harmful to real-life players in any way.

It's easy to get stressed, but you can remove all of this stress by knowing that nobody knows all of the rules by heart. Knowing all of the rules is an impossible feat unless you are some kind of robot. Have fun, let the players breathe, let yourself breathe, relax. It's just a game, and a really fun one at that, no matter what kind of TTRPG you are diving into.

Here are some other tips that I recommend.

You don't need to have an entire world created in the first session. You don't even need to have an entire world created at all. Many TTRPGs provide amazing pre-made adventures, concepts and ideas in the game box. It entirely depends on what you want to play. I personally love D&D and I've created a system that works. However, I fully understand that many people don't have the time or energy to invest in a game as wide open and immersive as that. The good thing is you are not alone and there are hundreds of alternatives out there. I have a list of twenty great TTRPGs to try that are not D&D. These are listed and reviewed in Chapter 5.

If you do try to run D&D and are feeling overwhelmed at the prospect of starting, I cannot stress enough how great the Starter Set is. It contains a condensed rule book and a pre-made adventure that is really fun and simple to follow. It also has pre-made character sheets which will save you a ton of time.

In my opinion, you should start out as small as you want to. I use a rule of three: have a setting, some information and an action. For example, have the players start at an inn, let the players hear some rumours, let the players fight something.

What are these rumours? Maybe someone vandalised a shop in town. Maybe someone is about to be executed (for your older players) or maybe mysterious lights have been seen on the edge of town the last few nights. I know what you're saying: 'I don't have anything ready for any of these adventures!'. You don't have to if you don't want to. A lot of rumours in real life turn out to be bogus. They could all be red herrings: the players investigate the lights, but they simply don't find them, so it could be something that you jot down and save for later. The vandalism has been done by some kids who have a hideout on the edge of town and who try to recruit the players to steal something with them – a slingshot from a shop or something; that's it, that's the quest. The goal is to have fun and let the players do the work by role-playing the scenario.

Your players may be shy at first, but in my experience it doesn't take long for them to come out of their shells and start discussing what to do, what routes to take and what they think is important.

I am a sucker for the following scenario. I have altered it a few times in the past but I think it's a good way to introduce the players to each other and to the mechanics of the game. The players start at an inn. Yes, that is the most clichéd thing in TTRPG history, but I personally love it. This may sound like I'm micro-managing, but if you do start at an inn and are playing with a younger audience, you should clarify that the inn or tavern they are at does not serve alcohol. If you don't, what may happen is you have a table full of 11-year-olds acting out being drunk, and you then may have to explain this to people around you, people who don't understand the world of TTRPGs. Not only that, it's common sense that they don't need to be engaging in this kind of thing, and it will make your life easier if you avoid it. This is just my opinion; if you're thinking this is me being a prude, that's perfectly fine.

Once the players are inside the inn, they should describe to the table, out loud, what the people in the inn would see as their character walks in. This is a good opportunity for players to describe their characters' features.

You will find that some younger players will spend a huge amount of time working on their character's appearance and backstory, and this moment provides an opportunity for them to show off what they've done. If a player only has five words to say about their character, that's fine too.

Once everyone has introduced themselves, I try to stay quiet, or just ask lightly what the players are doing: how are they interacting with the patrons, are they ordering food, are they going to decide to regale the room with a song or a story, are they going to try to overhear some gossip, whatever? I let them have fun with this. In my student group, one player spent time pickpocketing a burly looking half-orc while another played a game where they tried to toss a copper coin into the eye slit of a helmet that had been nailed to the wall. Let them roam around and get the feel of the place and get comfortable with each other's characters.

Then after a while, maybe an hour to two (in the game, not real-life time!), something or someone bursts into the inn and attacks the people within. I love a troll doing this, maybe because trolls in most TTRPGs can be tough to kill and are nine feet tall and scary. I love the idea of patrons at the inn scrambling to get away, the chaos of it. What it does is let the players experience combat right off the bat, because there will be players who are combat lovers. As a player, I am definitely someone who loves combat more than role playing, but as a GM I also love creating NPCs that interact with the players. This scenario allows players to figure out how to use their weapons and their abilities. Most likely they will all want to prove themselves as heroes and will want to take part in the fight. Once the fight has concluded, they can realise that they work well together and should team up. Maybe someone who witnessed the battle asks them to do a favour - find a lost item that was stolen, or maybe some friends of his who went missing on a fishing expedition, and he'll pay them each a hefty sum if they help to locate the missing item/friends. It's simply a good way to get the ball rolling and to let the players explore the area around them.

I feel that if you keep it simple you will feel less pressure in general. You can then build from there, create further story hooks for your players and go in incremental steps. In Chapter 3 I have discussed how to run TTRPGs on zero preparation.

You are also a player
Don't forget that as a GM you are part of the game, probably the most important part. What I mean by this is that you are a player like everyone else. Yes, you're there to ensure everyone has fun and is engaged (a very tricky job), but you're also a player and should be having fun too. If it's not

fun, you need to ask yourself why that is. Is it because you are worried about making a mistake? Are the players talking over you or to each other when they should be listening? If so, then you should try to take a step back and re-establish a few things. As far as making a mistake goes, as I've said, it doesn't really matter because it's your world and you can create it how you wish. I will discuss player behaviour expectations later in this chapter.

Are the players following the plan you had in your head? If your answer to this is 'no', that's a good thing! I love it when my players surprise me by deviating from the script I have in my head. Yes, it can be a bit of a rollercoaster ride, but there's nothing wrong with asking for a minute to collect yourself. Also, once you have been a GM for a little while, you will have a bank of ideas in your head that will be easy to plug into situations as they arise. Some of my most memorable moments have come when the players have completely gone off the tracks (see 'Embrace the chaos' below).

You need to enjoy the material

If you want your players to have fun, you also need to be having fun. If you want your players to be interested in the material, you need to be interested as well. If players see you in a good mood, they will typically follow suit (Make a Skill Check, 2021). For myself, I really enjoy seeing both comedy and horror-type elements in TTRPGs. It seems like a strange mix, but it works. I enjoy scaring the players to a degree. This will be discussed in the section below on Session Zero, but you as GM need to check on what your players are comfortable with. For myself, working with teens, I add a mixture of comedy and horror, ratcheting up the tension with foreboding clues, dreams and symbols. Then, out of the blue, they'll meet an NPC that makes them laugh, providing some relief. The students I work with really seem to latch onto this, and they themselves are hilarious, which also acts as a counter-balance to the atmosphere. Your job is to find the balance that works well with your players, their ages and their personalities.

You don't need to create an entire world

As a GM, you're not going to have time to build every nook and cranny of a world you are unleashing to your players. Fantasy author Brandon Sanderson discussed what's known as the Iceberg Theory of World-building. The world he creates is like a hollow iceberg: he does just enough to give the illusion to the reader that there's much more to discover, like a massive iceberg floating on the water, but at the same time the iceberg: is hollow (Make a Skill Check, 2021).

I love this analogy, and feel that I have been doing the same with my worldbuilding. What I do is provide enough small details to give that illusion. This might be a smell that greets players when they walk into a shop, a description of a few things on the shelves, a description of the shopkeeper and what they're wearing or the expression on their face. This is something your players may forget in ten seconds, but in that moment it makes it an immersive world. You will also have TTRPG 'stuff' crammed in your head over time that you can use to help you out. For example, very recently my players entered a library. I did not expect this; however, I had a few months ago run a library scenario with other players and therefore I quickly opened my notes from that session (another important factor: always try to take notes if you have time) and rattled off a few names of librarians and books that they might find.

I was also able to use the description of the library, how many people were in there and what the costs were for the services provided, all because I had taken notes. That said, it's still just a shell of a description, enough to make it interesting and engaging, with colourful characters that made the experience fun. Again, this is not something that has come instantly; I have been a GM for three years, which is a very short period of time, comparatively speaking – but I have kept notes and really enjoy building worlds.

You don't need to reinvent the wheel

There is so much material out there for building worlds in TTRPGs that you don't need to start from scratch. You can take inspiration from anyone. Websites like Drive-Thru RPG (which will be discussed in Chapter 5) contain thousands of pre-made adventures and settings, often at a very low price or even for free. There are also loads of Facebook Groups, Reddit channels and Twitter handles to follow, which will also be covered in more detail in Chapter 5.

What I hope you will take away from this section is that these worlds have already been set up for you. If you don't consider yourself a fantasy enthusiast, you can delve into the world of TTRPGs that take place in the modern era, or in outer space, or in another dimension that weirdly resembles our own. That is the beauty of these games; the possibilities are endless and once you find a resource, whether it's online or in a book or in person, you can mine its depths and take what you need from it.

Session Zero

Session Zero is simply the first session you have with your players. The point of a Session Zero is to establish many things. The following are what I establish early on. Sometimes these things need to be repeated, but it's a good idea to get them out of the way at the start.

The campaign

What kind of campaign are you going to run? Is it going to be one you have purchased (which I tend to do, more on those later) or is it going to be a homebrew adventure, one you've made entirely out of your own brain? If only I had the time to make my own homebrew adventures!

I currently have a 15-year-old in the library running their own homebrew adventures for students aged 11–13 and it is a huge amount of fun to watch. They do a ton of improvising (see 'Zero-preparation games' in Chapter 3) and they use the imagination of the players to help round out the scenarios.

Whatever you decide, it's a good idea to let players know early on. For example, I ran a TTRPG from September 2021 to July 2022 using one campaign module and by the end of it we had run 70 sessions on the nose. It was set in a jungle. Before we started I sat down with the teens and explained to them the setting. I told them very detailed things such as 'It's going to be a hot, humid place, there will be a lot of exploration happening, there will be a lot of dangerous animals, you *will* be bitten by bugs.' Things like that. This really affected the way the students created their characters. For example, one student decided to make their character someone who was from the jungle, a frog-like creature that would help the others navigate what is a very dangerous place!

This is why I encourage a Session Zero before the students even make their characters so you can help to establish their backstories, because in my opinion a player's backstory plays a huge role in the fun factor of a TTRPG.

Character creation

All you really need to know about this is to make it fun. My advice is to know how to create a character in the TTRPG that you are going to play, as this will save time and confusion. I have loads of students approaching me asking about making characters – some just love to do it.

'I make characters when I'm bored,' one 13-year-old player told me. They are always looking through the rule books, trying to roll up the fiercest player. This is a very fun part of playing TTRPGs. It became so popular in my library that I bought an extra copy of the book that involved character creation just so that students could access it from behind my desk and look up characters. I'm not saying that you need to go out and spend money like that – I only did it because I saw a very specific need. You can often create characters simply using pencils and scrap paper. Once you know the rules for character creation in the TTRPG you want to run, you can approach it in any way you want. Many TTRPGs have pre-made characters that will save you a lot of time and confusion, although it's a good idea to get to know how to do it in case it does come up.

There are many character-builder websites, depending on what TTRPG you want to play. If your players are specifically into D&D, you can find a fillable sheet in the D&D Media Gallery.[1] If you would like a more step-by-step builder that helps with choosing different classes and races, you could try the character builder in the Dungeon Master's Vault.[2]

Once the teens know what kind of setting they are going to be in, they make their own characters. I play a role in their backstories in that I know the main villains in the campaign; I know when the 'big' moments are going to take place. The fun of running a TTRPG happens, for me, when there's a big reveal or students discover things from their characters' past. This of course requires you to do some reading beforehand. There is a list of TTRPGs in Chapter 5 that will remove a lot of the work for you. These games often have pre-made adventures, characters and hooks that will do the work for you if you are short on time.

Once the players have their characters, I ask them to send me a copy of their character sheets. The kind of character sheets you have will depend on the TTRPG you are playing. However, all character sheets will contain information like name, race, abilities, background, personal history, equipment, spells (if applicable) and things such as health and appearance. Most of this information can be supplied from the imagination of the players. I ask for the character sheets because I can go over these to ensure that every player has filled theirs in correctly. It also helps me to learn about different types of characters. I don't pretend to know everything about every kind of character you can play in a TTRPG, so spending some time learning the rules around the characters will help the game to flow much better and is helpful for me down the line.

Having the character sheet also saves time in game if there's an instance where a player is unsure of some of the mechanics. Also, I can then tie in their backstories with the campaign I'm running and can ensure that they have some cool moments while playing. For example, a character in one of our campaigns always had dreams about a particular place and item. Throughout the campaign, I dropped hints about this place and item. Near the end of the campaign, they discovered that the item was crucial to the plot and needed to be destroyed. It was a big 'a-ha' moment for the players when the puzzle pieces all fell into place.

Knowing your players' characters, their backstories, strengths and weaknesses, will make for a much better game. However, be careful when creating an NPC or item that the players become very attached to, especially if you have in mind that that person, creature or item probably won't survive, as it could end up creating some hurt feelings. My advice is to understand the maturity level of your players, and you should be fine.

It's also a good idea to e-mail students anything particular about their characters and their ties to the campaign. This can also be done with handouts. I avoid telling them things in front of the other students because there are fun and interesting aspects to some characters that the teens might want to keep secret for a certain length of time, or the entire campaign.

To give an example, we had a character who knew that a family member had gone missing in the jungle. The player decided not to reveal this part of his backstory until much later in the game, when I dropped in clues about the missing person's whereabouts and it seemed that the team was getting close to finding them. Once discovered, the rest of the team wanted to send them on their way; but when it was revealed that the character was a long lost family member, this NPC spent the rest of the campaign with the team.

All of this relates back to making the game as immersive and fun as possible. If you show enthusiasm for players' characters and their stories, it will pay off in the end.

Table rules

Having a Session Zero is also essential for establishing the rules. I don't necessarily mean the rules of the actual game, but the unwritten rules of the table. I do have some specific rules and, because we've been playing together for so long, some of these don't need to be brought up. But it's important to set expectations right away.

These are the rules.

- Be kind to each other. This game is not an opportunity to be mean or to fight one another. I reinforce the idea that this is not a PvP game, and that it will rely on teamwork. I do not allow any PvP in my TTRPGs unless there's an instance where a character's mind has been taken over and it is woven organically into the story. Usually what happens if you allow players to fight each other is someone's feelings will get hurt, or players will gang up on one or two characters. I remind teens that there are plenty of other games that allow PvP, but this is a game where they will work together.

- Try to keep cross-talk to a minimum. This means when it's someone else's turn, be respectful and let them explain what they are doing without being interrupted or having other players talk over them. If players are continually talking over each other, it might work to have a turn system even when out of a combat situation. Simply start on your left and ask the player what they are going to do in this situation, then move clockwise around the table. This informal kind of turn taking for general scenarios will become the norm, and hopefully the players will adapt to it.

- Don't disrupt the game. If a player is being continually disruptive, either out of character or while they are role playing as a character, I suggest taking them aside after the game (or whenever you have time) and speaking to them about it without the other players present. It might be a simple, 'Hey, I want you to be a part of this and to have fun but we have five other players who also need to have their turn and speak their mind'. The player might not realise that they were being disruptive; they might simply have been getting caught up in the fun. They might, on the other hand, decide over time that the play style of a TTRPG is not for them after all - it happens.

- No dice spinning. I ask the players not to do this, otherwise they will have a tendency to spin the multi-sided dice all over the table and I've found that it becomes a huge distraction for everyone. Yes, they are there to have fun; but trust me, they will have more fun if they listen and engage with what's going on. Also, the dice inevitably end up on the floor, which causes delays, and time is always an issue. It could simply be a bugbear for me and no one else cares about dice spinning, but I find it annoying and distracting.

Session Zero is also a time to ask the players what they want to get from the game. This will help you to tailor it to their liking. As already mentioned, I do use purchased campaigns because I don't have time to make my own. That said, tailoring them to the students' likes is important and easily doable - it just requires you to do some reading beforehand.

Before a session

I want to emphasise that you have set up a TTRPG to have fun, not to be stressed. All things considered, playing these games is supposed to be cathartic for not only the students but yourself. I try to remember this at all times, especially when I find myself stressing about not having enough material ready or worried that I have forgotten something important. It happens. You can be running TTRPGs for 30 years and forget basic rules, but that's the beauty of them: you are, more often than not, given a lot of flexibility within the world to bend the rules to fit the personalities sitting at the table in front of you.

Even if you are holding a pre-written story, it doesn't mean you have to follow it word for word. I cannot remember how many times the students have engaged in actions that have forced me to abandon the plot altogether and just go with what they have in mind, which has frequently been more fun. Sure, you can always find ways to tie it back into the main plot, and I think you should try to do this if possible, but don't worry if things don't go according to your meticulous plans.

Another thing to keep in mind: the players are the ones who make the world what it is. Yes, you have created towns and villages and terrifying dungeons, but without the players interacting with those things the game is nothing. The players make the story. It's their story to tell, while you provide situations for them to deal with and see what happens. That's the fun of it.

The following is a brief example.

The adult players in a fantasy-based TTRPG I was running were camping far from the main road because they were paranoid about being followed. It was spring and they were near the north, so it was cold – but the air was clear and sound was carrying.

I decided to have a covered horse-drawn wagon travelling along the road, heading north. One player was able to hear it, but from the distance (and because of poor rolling) they couldn't make anything out, other than that there was a horse pulling a covered wagon.

Now, the players could have just said 'We'll let it go', and that would have been that; the wagon would have been gone forever. If you had written something really special about that horse or if the wagon had been filled with treasure or crazed goblins or something, you might have felt a little slighted as a GM – but it's not your place to railroad the players into investigating. In such a case, my advice is if you have written something really cool that you think they'd enjoy, save it for another random encounter later on.

However, in my case, my players did want to investigate. I did not have treasure or a horde of enemies hiding in the wagon – I had nothing. It was an empty wagon being pulled by a horse, and as GMs we are not required to provide any further information. Again, my players could have just let the horse carry on and never be seen again, but one player unhitched it and took the horse as their own. They gave it a name, fed it and cared for it. They had that horse for a very long time throughout the campaign and it turned out that I had to write some pretty fun stuff around that horse to make the campaign more dangerous and thrilling for that character. Conclusion? The players make the story.

My approach before a session is to familiarise yourself with the game. I mean this in two ways. You need to read up on the rules of the game and on the game itself, but also immerse yourself in the setting that you are going to place the players in. This makes it much more fun for everyone when you get started.

Once you've had your first few sessions, there are other things that you will need to consider. Ask yourself: what possible actions will the teens take in the next session or two, or what should I be prepared for? If I know the students are going to meet an important NPC, I make notes on what the outcomes might be. For instance, if they decide to attack the character, how will it react? Will it fight back? If so, I will need to know all of its abilities, spells and behaviours that will make the encounter seem authentic. Will the players mine this NPC for information? If so, how much should I give? This depends on the NPC's abilities, but I want to have a bank of information at the ready.

This same advice goes for a place. You don't need to have every single cobblestone alleyway memorised or written down, but in my opinion you should have important places at the ready, as well as red herrings. Not every place the players visit needs to be related to their main quest, and not every person they meet needs to be vital to the story. Sometimes the guy selling trinkets from a cart on the road is just a guy selling trinkets. Sure, he may have heard a few rumours that will send the players down a specific path, but it doesn't mean he's honest or holding correct information at all.

This is what makes it fun for me – making a world where there are 'real' kinds of people: people going about their everyday business and not really caring what the players' quest is. I think the players enjoy this as well, like when they approach a random person in the inn and ask about their quest and that person has no idea what they're talking about and just wants to get on with their meal.

Of course, this means that you'll have to do some writing or find pre-generated NPCs or shops. There are several websites that have these, and many pre-made campaigns have NPCs, places and rumours that will help you greatly.

What if you find yourself caught short? If a player asks you, 'What's that person's name?' or says, 'I want to ask them about the lost treasure in the mountain', you can simply make something up. Pick a name off the top of your head; say that they tell the players they are too busy to talk or rudely walk away. In other words, just try to make it realistic.

If possible, set up your tables, dice, screens and maps (if you have them) before the session starts (Figure 4.1). You might not think this is a big deal, but setting up does eat into your time and, as we discussed, time is your enemy when running a game in a school or public library. Have snacks if you allow that kind of thing; in the public library it was guaranteed that we would have snacks.

Figure 4.1 *Table set up for start of play*

Tips for a GM during a session

Encourage the players' success. This is something I had to learn the hard way when I first became a GM. Your job is not to kill the players; your job is to create a world full of danger and watch them succeed. The trick is to make it hard enough to make it a thrill but not too easy that it's boring. Easier said than done, I know, but it's a balancing act that you will achieve over time.

Don't get caught up in the small stuff – 'Wait, you can't cast that Sleep spell, you didn't buy the necessary rose petal ingredients when you were in Ogretown!' When you're dealing with a time crunch in a school or public library, stuff like this can kill a session quickly. The point is to let the students have fun and be creative. Once you've read through the rules of the TTRPG you are going to play, work within that framework and bend the rules if needed.

'You can try', is the motto of famous YouTube GMs – but it is a good motto in my opinion. A GM shouldn't really say 'no' if a student is playing a character who genuinely wants to try something that is fun and interesting. Even if it's something you think is impossible in the game, they can try, they can roll the dice and find out how difficult it is. As I've said previously, as long as it isn't offensive, rude or harmful to other players, you should let them try it out.

Avoid re-rolling for maximum effect. What I mean by this is, let's say a student asks to pick a lock; they fail the roll but they say, 'Ok, I just want to keep re-rolling till I do it'. If you allow this, there's no point in them rolling at all. There should be consequences for failing a check like this – they break their lock pick, they make a sound and alert an enemy, they trigger a trap or they even break the lock so that it can't be picked anymore. This is especially true for knowledge checks: either a player knows something or they don't – they can't keep re-rolling and then suddenly they understand the entire history of Blagorth and his Quaggoth underlords from the Lantern Spire of Alamardia. Each TTRPG you play will have different rules on what the players can and cannot do, but in my experience if you make things *too* easy, it quickly becomes boring.

Sessions will need to be fast paced; that's just the way it works in a school or public library. You simply don't have time to get bogged down in the minutiae of the rules or the setting. Therefore it's important that you begin the sessions as if you are reading a passage from a novel: make it dramatic, make it funny, but don't make it like you're reading from a manual on lawnmowers. Pre-written campaigns will often have text boxes for you to read aloud that add drama and flourish to your games, but it's easy and fun to make up your own based on what your players did in the session before. The point is that you need to move fast, and giving a quick recap or introduction to their situation will help set the tone. To simplify things, you could put three main points on a flipchart or whiteboard so that when players come to the game they can quickly read through the recap and get ready. It doesn't have to be full of detail.

My advice is to save recaps and longer information for e-mails. I e-mail the students as a group after every session to give them a recap of what just happened, just in case there was any confusion. This can be done once a week, or even once every two weeks if you are pressed for time. Use a few short bullet points to keep players in the loop (especially if any missed a session) and to ensure that they are ready to go in the next session. This may be difficult in a public library session, where you may see different players on a weekly or even daily basis.

I think the students enjoy reading the recaps, as I try to include anything funny that happened, which is almost every day. (I am in the process of writing a novel based on my current students' adventure in the jungle based entirely on the decisions they have made. I hope to give it to them before they leave school as a 'thank you' for all of the amazing hours we've spent playing RPGs in the library.)

Even more important, in the e-mail I include any loot or treasure the students may have discovered. Yes, you can do this in person, but if you stand there and explain the fine details of a magical item to one player, the others might zone out or, worse, the player themselves might forget. It's important, therefore, to e-mail the players the loot they have discovered after a particularly hard fight or puzzle and add it to a loot tracker. What's a loot tracker? It's simply a document I share with the students detailing all of the loot they have found since session one, including money. I also list who has what and what the effects of those items are.

The following is an example of a loot tracker organised in alphabetical order – just so the players can find things more easily. I list the names of the characters at the end so they know who has each item.

Loot tracker

Cloak, dark blue and embroidered with gold stars: Non-magical. Moira

Letter from the Witch Valley Hags detailing their plans to overthrow the land. Francis

Map of Kalook Valley. Skov

Ring, crimson red in colour: Magical, allows you to jump 60 feet in the air. Wotah.

It's as simple as that and can be placed in a shared document. If I've forgotten anything, players can e-mail me and let me know so that I can add it in. If a player finds a particularly complicated magical item that has multiple benefits or effects, I will print off the detail and give it to them so they can staple it into their notebook or add it to their existing sheets.

Other advice is to let the players describe what their characters are doing, which makes it much more fun for everyone and gives you a break as the GM. Allow players at the table to describe how they kill the monster or how they leap across the chasm to escape from a rock fall. TTRPGs are all about imagination, and giving players a voice to express themselves is key.

As mentioned in Chapter 3, displaying the turn order can be a lifesaver. If you have particularly rambunctious players, having a turn order, even when out of combat, can be helpful. It ensures that everyone gets a chance to have input into what's going on. Inevitably, you are going to have some players who are shy and some who will try to dominate the table. It's important to let everyone have a chance to express themselves and have fun with their characters.

Start with a bang

You may have a lot of backstory ready, or a long monologue or a wordy introduction, but I would save all of that for later. My preference is to get the players into a combat situation early. It will set the tone and make things a lot of fun for everyone. In addition, it will help the players to learn how to use their characters and familiarise themselves with the different rules of the game.

Are your characters on a ship? Have it get attacked by a giant sea turtle that eats money; make the players dump their money into its mouth to avoid the ship being destroyed.

Are your characters walking along a road? Have them get ambushed by goblins who are hiding in a destroyed wagon.

Are your characters meeting in an inn? Have a brawl break out; maybe a creature emerges from the basement and the characters have to save the day, gaining favour from the owners and stumbling upon a mystery in the basement.

Whatever the scenario or environment, it will be much more rewarding if you start the players off with something exciting and without getting bogged down in the minutiae of the game. In my experience, students are really itching to go and fight something, or they are itching to go and explore and to meet NPCs to build the world around them. Either way, let them explore, go with the flow and have fun.

Embrace the chaos

This doesn't mean that you let things get out of hand. What I mean is that when students discover that most TTRPGs are open world creations where their characters can explore and interact with everything, expect the unexpected and go with it. Sometimes the most memorable events happen when your best-laid plans are destroyed by a player's actions.

Here is an example.

I had prepped a few encounters with our students who were playing a TTRPG where, the session before, they had secured passage on an airship with a group of NPC adventurers. In my mind, the voyage on the airship was going to be short and sweet. What ended up happening was entirely different. The students simply needed to go from point A to point B so that the plot line I had written out could advance.

As they were up in the air on the deck of the airship, one student, who was playing a wizard, asked:

'What do I see?'
Me (not really having anything prepared): 'Uh, nothing much, you see some birds flying alongside you about 40 feet away.'
'Oh cool, well, we are low on rations so I'm going to try and catch one for supper. I'll roast it with my fire-bolt spell as they come near.'
Me: 'Sure, you'd have to roll an attack like normal, though.'
The student rolls the lowest possible roll in the game.

Now, when students in TTRPGs roll low, and I mean really, really low, there need to be consequences to those actions. In this case, the player is trying to send a line of fire at a flock of birds, knowing that she is standing less than ten feet from the billowing sail of an airship. Sure, as GM you can say 'you miss', but this negates the point of the entire game because the fun of it is that super-high rolls mean great success and super-low rolls mean horrible, horrible failure.

Me: 'You stumble as you cast your spell, your hands go in the air and the fire erupts from your fingers and sets the sail alight! It goes up like parchment paper, the crew are screaming, frantically trying to put it out with whatever water they have on board.'

Now was the time for another student, playing a character whose backstory was that they were an orphan who survived by honing their thieving skills, to say:

'While they are distracted, I'm going to go down below deck and see what I can find.'
Me (still nothing prepped about the layout of the ship or what items are below): 'Uh, sure, you go down and you see a bunch of foot lockers laid out by some hammocks.'
'Oooh, nice! I'm going to try and open them.'

Me: 'They are locked.'
'No problem, I use my lock picks and try to open them.'
Me: 'Ok, roll to see if you unlock them.'
Student rolls really well and takes a couple of potions, gold and silver.
'Ok, I'm going to go back up, but I'm going to sneak.'
Me: 'No problem, you'll have to roll to sneak back up so no one notices you.'
The student rolls the worst possible roll.
Me: 'You trip going up the steps, the items you stole spill out onto the deck, one of the crewmen shouts, you look up and you see smoke and flames engulfing the ship, a huge man with tattoos covering his arms leers down at you. "What do you think you're doing?!" he asks. Then he shouts at the others that you are stealing their stuff. Meanwhile, the sails are eaten up by the flames and the airship begins to tilt to the side.'
Another student asks: 'Does this ship have a harpoon on it?'
Me: 'Yes, yes it does.'
'I'm going to go up there and fire the harpoon at the tattoo guy that's threatening us.'
Me: 'Uh, ok, you can run up there, it's going to be tricky with the way the ship is tilting but you can try.'

Student runs up to the harpoon and rolls an attack. The attack roll is, once again, so low I have to have consequences.

Me: 'The harpoon misses wildly, it strikes the mast of the ship, bringing the entire structure down onto the deck, the ship is going down!'

The students then try valiantly to save the ship but there's not a lot they can do. The ship crashes into the deep forest, some of them are badly wounded and half the party is separated from the rest. The crash and resulting fire also attracts a roaming bandit group who are looking for trouble. The students then spend many more sessions trying to get out of the forest, avoid the bandits, find their missing party members, repair the airship, run from the crew who survived the crash, plus try to find the path to the main quest that they were seeking in the first place.
    All because I said, 'You see some birds.'

This was chaotic, and a bit stressful as I had to be on my toes, but it is a moment the students still talk about more than a year later. I wasn't prepared, but I didn't stop them from acting, and yes, I even helped things along a little bit by making their poor rolls have disastrous consequences. The important thing is to have a balance. Trust me when I say the students were howling with laughter at their terrible rolls. If I had seen that they were genuinely upset by anything, I would have softened the results somewhat, but that is the reality of playing TTRPGs: bad rolls often mean that bad things happen. The good thing is that the students will have the story to remember and they can even include it in their character sheets so they don't forget it.

Teen GMs

I strongly recommend allowing your teens to run their own TTRPG programmes. At the time of writing, I have a 15-year-old student who runs D&D twice a week for an amazing group of students whose ages range from 11 to 13. Our teen GM volunteered to take charge in light of the very high demand we were experiencing to run TTRPGs.

The following is my advice when having teen GMs.

Use pre-written material

Our teen GM shuns all pre-written material and makes things up in their head, furiously writing in their notebook all the ideas that they unleash on players. The student players love their GM and never, ever miss a session. One time our teen GM was ill and I took over. I was reminded that the players prefer the teen's GM style over mine – which was something I actually loved to hear! However, I think overall that pre-written material will really help to reduce anxiety on the part of your teen GM, especially if they are new to it. Once your GM has a few sessions under their belt, then it can be time for them to launch into the homebrew (homemade) material. My advice is to check in with them regularly to ensure that they aren't feeling overwhelmed or anxious about being a GM. Think back to rule number one: having fun. If the GM isn't having fun, it's guaranteed that no one at the table will be, either.

Give them freedom

I am very fortunate in that I know the players and the GM well, therefore if I step away from the table for a few minutes to handle something else, everything will continue like clockwork. The players are there to play and the GM has it under control. However, if you are feeling anxious about leaving the game to run by itself, you should ask yourself why this is. If it's because the players are being unruly, it is not the teen's responsibility to reign them back in. If it's because the teen hasn't had time to prep a scenario, you can quickly hand them one, which is why it's a good idea to have *something* prepared, even if it's a place and a few people, a jobs board with three little quests on it, a missing cat, a person who's gone missing in the sewer, someone who needs to have their lost polar bear figurine found – anything!

Also, it may be instinctive on your part to hang around or get involved, which is fine for the first few sessions; but once you feel that the teen has a handle on it, my advice is to let them have freedom to take it where they want it to go, whether they are following the rules to the letter or not. My approach is to help set everything up and to 'check in' every ten minutes or so to ensure that everything is going smoothly. I act as a rule finder for the teen, in that if something comes up that could potentially bog the game down, I tell them to keep things running while I look up the rule. It's like having a shadow GM who just helps keep everything from slowing down. I also really enjoy going around the table and looking at the players' character sheets and helping new players to create characters, no matter what kind of TTRPG it is.

Be encouraging

This probably doesn't need to be said, but it's very important that the teen GM feels encouraged to create the world that they have in their mind. I will offer to help make handouts or print off images for them to give to their players. I print off creature statistics or anything that I think will help them to make their game fun, fast and engaging. The rule of 'you can try' applies to the GM as well, and I feel that having someone to encourage them to keep going is crucial. The amazing thing about TTRPGs is that failure doesn't mean the end of the world; it means that something funny or ridiculous might happen, or they may find themselves in hot water. In my experience, many of the student players actually *enjoy* sometimes rolling terribly if it means that their teen GM is going to launch into a descriptive narrative of how horribly they have failed. In a safe, inclusive environment, failure is just another aspect of the game and it can be a lot of fun. I want the teen GM to come into the library knowing that this is a programme that belongs to them and their players. I am simply giving them the space to create a cool world and unleash it on their friends.

Help to organise

What do I mean by this? I want to encourage the players to keep track of their progress, their successes and failures, their amazing moments and whatever else they want to capture. When all is said and done, this game is about creating positive memories with their friends and being in the library.

You do not have to spend a lot of money on journals or diaries for the players to keep their ideas in place. In our library we have a scrap paper drawer that many students use to draw characters (Figure 4.2 on the next page) or scribble down ideas. These can be hole punched or stapled together for them to keep in their journal or binders.

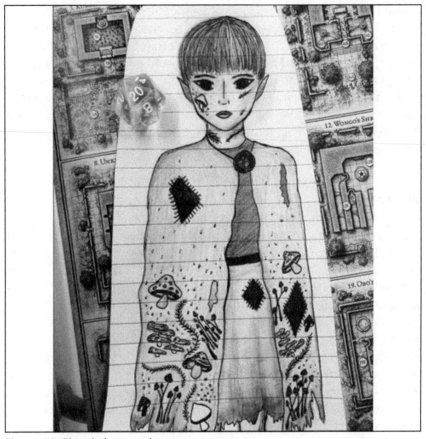

Figure 4.2 *Player's character drawn on scrap paper*

I see our student players carrying around their battered journals full of notes, illustrations, player stats, magical items and backstories on a daily basis, and it fills me with joy every time. For teen GMs, these journals can be a life saver. I have a journal filled with my TTRPG ideas and it saves me a great deal of time and headache every week, knowing that I have this base of information at the ready. If you encourage your teen GM to take notes, write stories, build worlds, their players will benefit greatly, and so will they.

Summary

It may seem like there's a lot to do both before and during a session. The best advice I can give is to try a few sessions with a low number of players (maximum six) and see how you do. There are a lot of TTRPGs out there that make things like character creation and world building extremely easy, almost in a choose-your-own-adventure style. These are listed in more detail in Chapter 5, where what I hope to get across is that there is a very high chance that the youth you serve, either in the public or school library, will probably think that TTRPGs with massive worlds and overwhelming rules like D&D are the only game in town. Once they realise that there are dozens, if not hundreds, of alternatives, they will most likely never look back.

Notes

1   https://media.wizards.com/2016/dnd/downloads/5E_CharacterSheet_
    Fillable.pdf
2   www.dungeonmastersvault.com/pages/dnd/5e/character-builder

5 TTRPGs for Your Library and Further Resources

Introduction

This chapter has four sections. The first section is a list of 20 great TTRPGs that you can try in your public or school library. I've also included some one-page RPGs with descriptions and links to them. The second section contains a list of online resources that you might find useful when starting a TTRPG. The third section is a recommended reading list of other guides that may be helpful in creating engaging and immersive worlds in your TTRPG. The fourth section is a list of fiction books that can be promoted to children aged 9+ who are fans of TTRPGs.

TTRPG list

The price of TTRPGs varies according to the size and scope of the game. Larger TTRPGs often require multiple books and add-ons to be purchased whereas smaller TTRPGs sometimes only require one book or one item to download. In many cases, the rules for these games constitute one to four pages. Many of these are also aimed at younger players who might find larger-scope TTRPGs overwhelming.

Amazing Tales
Great for ages four and up, this is an amazing introduction to TTRPGs. All of the rules are on one page. Players can create a character and are provided a limited number of skills. Each skill is represented by a different dice. To determine success or failure, you roll the dice that is relevant to the skill needed. You only need to roll a three or higher to succeed. Thinking of the age range, this is perfect: it keeps the action moving swiftly and you are not bogged down. The book that comes with the game is essentially a guide on how to keep things interesting for kids: a collection of tips for new GMs on how to run a TTRPG, which is extremely useful. The settings are

immersive, full of talking animals and fairy lands, to name just a few. It's a brilliant TTRPG, and the book itself is worth any price!

Andor
A family-friendly adventure game to help a wolf find her three cubs. There is a ticking-time element, as a dragon is descending upon your city. You can play between four different heroes. You play with six-sided dice, but they have images on them rather than the usual dots. You are given side quests or tasks before you can find the wolf cubs for the wolf. You have a specific number of actions to do during the day; then the game turns to night, when you get more actions. Random tokens placed on the board represent monsters or magical items, or even gold coins to buy stuff! To prevent the dragon from entering the town you have to defeat monsters. There are D&D-style classes that have different dice and abilities. This is a fun, fast-paced game that your family will love!

Dungeon!
Dungeon! could be classified more as a board game than a TTRPG, but I'm including it because of its close ties with D&D and TTRPGs in general. Fun, fast and competitive, it will introduce the concept of D&D to younger players without breaking the bank or relying on complex rules. The idea is simple: you choose a character with all their stats pre-made. You get to move this character a certain number of squares per turn. Your goal is to get as much loot as you can and return to the entrance before the other players. Seems simple, right? Wrong! There are monsters hiding behind almost every door, and if you lose your fight against them there's a big chance you'll lose some of your hard-earned loot. It's a race to the finish that is a lot of fun. The only possible drawback is the time it takes to set up the tokens, and sometimes pieces get lost, as they are small. However, if you are wanting to introduce young players to the concept of a TTRPG, you can't go wrong with this game.

Dungeon Mayhem
This is more of a TTRPG card game, but it's too fun not to include in this list. I recommend it for players aged nine and up. You choose a character from a base of cards. Each character has pre-written strengths and abilities. There is no dice rolling; rather, you play a series of cards to try to kill your opponents. You have a health meter that goes up and down depending on the damage you take and what you do during your turn. There is a lot of humour to the game and it's very fast paced. In my experience, some younger players can get upset over being 'piled on' by others, so it's crucial

that you enforce the turn order! It's an easy game to learn and there are a few expansion sets available that make it much more engaging.

Golden Sky Stories
Based in Japan, this is a beautifully made game that harks back to films like *Spirited Away*. There are no dice to roll, and it is stripped down and easy to run. Each character can inhabit four different attributes; characters each have three resources that can increase their attributes, and dreams that can aid them. The game discourages violence on all levels; characters are penalised for fighting or causing others harm. It is a very stylised game and its primary goal is to relax and let students create their own stories. If you have teens or children who simply want to immerse themselves in a story where they use their characters' personalities to drive the story rather than violence, killing or conquering, this is a game you should definitely check out.

Hero Kids
An amazing game aimed at ages four to ten, this is a huge blast to play. It's fairly inexpensive and has a lot of great options for everyone. What's great about Hero Kids is that the game's complexity can be adapted for different age ranges, which is something that's hard to do with other TTRPGs. The rule book has only four pages and you use only standard six-sided dice. There's not a lot of adding or subtracting, which is aimed well at those younger players! There's also no 'death' per se: monsters run away from the good guys or they simply get knocked out cold. Your character cannot die, there is no TPK (Total Party Kill); instead, helpful townsfolk bring you to their village to help you rest if everyone in your group gets knocked out. This is a standard fantasy TTRPG with Viking themes. There are no adults; the kids are left in charge and of course mayhem ensues! The children's job is to protect the village from any bad guys. The combat rules are very simple: highest roll wins, easy! All adventurers have three points of health and, when hit, defenders take one point of damage. It's a game you'll be playing within minutes, learning the rules quickly and sticking with it for a long time!

Kids on Bikes
Aimed at ages 11+ this is a must for anyone who has *Stranger Things* fans in their library. Set in the 1980s, it is full of 80s references and is reminiscent of *The Lost Boys*, *The Monster Squad*, *Stand By Me*, *The Goonies* and so on. You play a child, a teen or an adult and have to list their greatest fear. You also list what motivates them, trying to ensure it matches the age

of the character you are creating. You also add flaws and strengths for your character. Instead of rolling dice to determine your stats, you assign different dice, like d8s, d10, d12s etc. that you roll when you are called upon to use that particular stat. The stats include Grit, Charm, Strength and so on. There is a free book on the website to help build characters, and the game itself provides some great ones. The world that is created is much more collaborative than in other TTRPGs, the main rule being that it is a world before mobile/cell phones and the town should be pretty small. The book provides questions that you should answer with your players to determine what kind of town you are building, which is a very unique approach and should get the players excited about getting involved! Players also contribute rumours about the town.

Legacy of Dragonholt

Dragonholt is a choose-your-own-adventure style of playing set in a role-playing world that does not need a GM. You can play by yourself or with five other friends. The rules are just two pages long, starting with a scenario setting, followed by step-by-step instructions that tell you how to play the game from the very beginning. You can use a pre-made character or make one from scratch using the sheets that come with the game. What I like about the game is that when you meet an NPC, the book gives you options for how you interact with them. The writing is of an extremely high quality, the interactions are very deep and the book moves seamlessly from one section to the next. The book also helps you to track the passage of time, which then forces you to move to different parts of the book. It's a lovely game that has some very interesting quests, side quests and room to grow.

Little Monster Detectives

Aimed at ages four and up and beautifully illustrated, this game is designed to bring younger players into TTRPGs while helping them to conquer their fears. The book is about 100 pages long and centres on exploration and imagination. The world is full of monsters: they might be under the bed, in the closet or down the street. The game places children in the shoes of detectives who seek out these monsters and trap them in a glass jar. The jar is then brought to The Agency, who turn the monsters into friendly creatures that are not frightening. The game was written by child psychologists and encourages players to play the game using co-operation and roaming around the garden or the house to play. There are real-life rewards like bravery stickers that the children can win.

Little Wizards

Little Wizards is aimed at ages six and up and is set in the magical land of Coinworld. Players can be mages and sorcerers, but aren't limited to this – there is a lot of choice when it comes to character creation, which young players will really get their teeth into. Players can choose which abilities their characters will exceed at. Here, the great thing is that characters are limited to three traits, which reduces time and confusion when it comes to making a cool character. The game mechanics are streamlined and easy to follow. Players roll 2d6 (two six-sided dice) to determine their actions and their fate. Rolling double ones means a critical failure, whereas rolling double sixes results in an overwhelming success. Even better, as they progress, players gain points that they can spend on new abilities and cool traits. There are three adventures in the book for the GM to unleash. This is another amazing TTRPG aimed at a young audience that won't confuse or confound the players or the adults.

Magical Kitties Save the Day

Aimed at ages six and up and taking around one hour to play, Magical Kitties is a really fun family adventure game. It is light on rules, fast and easy to play, and character creation is extremely fast. You can play this game with two younger ones and an adult GM, and it probably works best if you have at least two players. The game helps to describe character (or kitty) creation in a very clear and easy to understand way. Your kitties are cute, cunning or fierce. You can also have different talents, flaws and magical powers. The kitties also have a human companion – the game has pre-made humans or you can make your own. Your injury levels range from 'owies' to actual damage. The adult GM needs to choose different levels of difficulty. The game uses six-sided dice, so there are no complications or wasted time looking for many different kinds of dice. The adventure supplied is full of references to great books and great hooks that keep the adventure going. The main adventure book comes with a beautiful map and lots of different paths that the players can take. The back of the book contains a completed adventure where the kitties save a library – nothing could be better than that! There is also an adventure comic book where readers choose their own path. Great stuff!

Monster Slayers

Monster Slayers is a D&D game for ages six and up and is FREE to download![1] Each adventure is about 15 pages long with rules constituting three pages. All you need to play are five or six people, pencils and paper, one d20 and one d6, along with scissors to cut out the tokens. The heroes are pre-made and are from the D&D world of fighters, wizards and so forth. There's a lot of combat, which six-year-olds like, a lot of laughs, and it's super easy to get started. The game is perfect if you are short on time and budget and have a young audience you'd like to introduce D&D to without completely overwhelming them.

My Little Pony: Tales of Equestria RPG
With My Little Pony character sheet templates and even a 'close your eyes and choose' dice-roll page for those who don't have multi-sided dice, this is a great game for younger TTRPG players. It is simply laid out and is promoted as a storytelling game. The rules are streamlined and user-friendly. Friendship is the primary theme here, and stands above all of the other stats. There is a lot of fun to be had with this game, and the monsters you fight are really cool, like Mohawk, the hawk with an attitude. What's even cooler is that there is a mini-guide inside for new GMs - perfect for a teen in your library hoping to play TTRPGs with a new audience.

No Thank You, Evil!
Set in the land of Storia, No Thank You, Evil! (NTYE) is aimed at ages five and up. It is much more accessible than a typical D&D campaign, which is usually suitable for ages 11+ (but D&D can be tweaked for much younger audiences as well). Players create characters using cards - and, of course their own imagination, but the cards do a lot of the work for you, which greatly decreases the amount of time it takes to create a character, compared to other TTRPGs. Character stats are fun and straightforward, and range from Tough to Smart, Fast and Awesome. Special abilities and inventory are pre-written, which again, for a younger audience, is perfect.

You also get to choose companions, which constitute another set of cards. The game comes with three pre-written encounters which bring the game to life in a fun and easy way, especially for anyone new to the TTRPG world. World encounters include pirates, dinosaurs, robots, a time machine and much more. There's even a curse amusement park with ghosts and zombie (but not scary) teddy bears. Like D&D, the GM tells the story and players interact with the story, rolling a six-sided dice to see what happens to their characters. What's great about NTYE is that players can spend points to help their friends to achieve their goals. There's much fun to be had, and tons of different possibilities. Players can also make their characters stronger (and richer) by defeating enemies and finishing quests. It's got a lot of D&D to it without any of the complicated rules. Like D&D, there is no real ending, so if you've got a creative GM it could go on for ages, making it a really fun and engaging programme.

Pugmire

In a world where humans no longer exist and dogs have evolved to speak and walk upright, each race represents a different breed of dog with different abilities. It looks like a traditional D&D-style game with a GM screen that you place in front of you as you run the game. The screen has a ton of stats and information on it for you to use as a quick reference. The book that comes with this game is 254 pages, so it is a bit more complex than other TTRPGs on this list. However, all of the rules and character creation are in this one book, which is a huge reduction on other traditional TTRPGs. The rules are also easier to comprehend and kids aged 11+ will have a great time creating their characters.

Ryuutama

Published initially in Japan, easy on rules and based on the theme of travel, this is a TTRPG that immerses you in the world of dragons. It does require the GM to add some flourish to the world. Players are expected to go on a journey. Dragons are NPCs that step in to help the players. There are seven different classes, each one having three different skills and four different stats. The game uses four-, six-, eight- and ten-sided dice for the most part. This is a game that is heavy on storytelling. If you as a GM have some time to sink into it, there are a heap of charming elements to the game. It does rely on a lot of role playing, so if you have students who are somewhat introverted it might be a struggle. It is kid friendly and does not inflict a lot of stress on the GM, as there are a wealth of crib sheets and support. If you have a lot of imagination at your table and want a heart-warming story to replace dungeon-crawling violence, this is for you!

Quest

What's great about Quest is that it doesn't overwhelm new players, yet at the same time it offers a lot of immersive gameplay. Players still get to do a lot of creative work in making their own characters with backstories and goals, along with cool abilities and equipment (12 items or less!). Character introductions are fun and allow for a lot of flexibility. The rules are simplified and easy to follow. Players roll a 20-sided dice to determine their fate, but the rule book helps you to determine the specific fate, which is a dream for any GM who doesn't have time to develop an entire scenario in their mind in two minutes. The dice system is extremely easy to comprehend and ensures a high level of success, which again makes life easier for everyone. New GMs rejoice! You do not have to have a lot of experience to start this game: you receive a profile of your world with tons of starters to keep everything rolling smoothly.

Starport
Starport is set in a fantasy world aimed at ages five and up. What is great about it is that it relies on non-violence and focuses on storytelling and being imaginative. The GM can be an adult or even an older teen, as it is a fun and simple introduction to TTRPGs. It uses a 20-sided dice for players to determine if they succeed at different things. This could be helping a robot friend, leaping over a hole or climbing a wall – whatever. Players must roll over a preset number depending on what action they are trying to accomplish. This is very similar to D&D except that, as mentioned, it is a non-violent version. The guide can determine the number as long as it does not go above 25. Players get four main traits: Toughness, Sneakiness, Smartness and Helpfulness. They gain levels in these four traits and are given tokens depending on what level they are at. So, for example, a player is trying to solve a puzzle; they roll a ten on the 20-sided dice, and they can spend a token to try to solve the puzzle if the GM has set the number higher than ten. Throughout the quest, players acquire coins and can get pets. There is also cool loot like hover boards and superglue. There are three quests included in the game book for new GMs to use with their players. This is a great game with a low difficulty setting, which teaches role playing and does not contain violence.

Stuffed Fables
Aimed at ages seven and up, players take the form of stuffed animals belonging to a little girl – these go on an adventure while she is asleep. The box contains seven adventures, each adventure taking between an hour and an hour and a half to play. The spiral-bound book also acts as the map and contains the stuffed animals' objective for each map page. The game is played entirely with six-sided dice, all of different colours. The colours represent different things, like attacks and movement. Combat is easy and currency comes in the form of buttons! Creature cards are bright, clear and easy to understand. There are cool pieces of loot and equipment to find. This is a great, loveable story and the goal is to make it to the end of the story – simple and fun!

Tiny Dungeon
Tiny Dungeon comes in a small book that is super easy to understand. Your character sheet can be fitted onto a revision or recipe card, and the rules need reading just once. Players tell the GM what they want to do. They roll two six-sided dice and if they get a five or a six on either dice it is considered a success. Simple! In combat, you score one point for damage to your opponent. There are other rules that require rolling, but they all

involve the six-sided dice. Casting a spell is easy too, rolling in the same manner as above. You do not have to understand spell levels or slots like in D&D. This is great for kids who find the spell slot system in larger TTRPGs too difficult to comprehend. Instead of levels, you gain traits. There are great charts in the book for the GM to create monsters or quest hooks. There are also tons of dinosaurs that have really cool features and attacks. There's even an adventure generator with different settings and events that will save you a lot of time. The pre-made quests are based on such things as the film *Labyrinth* and *Game of Thrones*.

One-page RPGs

One-page RPGs are, simply put, TTRPGs where the entire plot and rules can fit on one page. There are tons of them, some free, some with a small associated cost. These are perfect for anyone who has very little time or wants to introduce younger players to TTRPGs. Keep in mind that many of the one-page RPGs have adult themes, but the good thing is that it won't take you long to read through the content!

D&D-ish
A short and sweet TTRPG system that strips away all hefty details and focuses solely on how to play the game. Everything else is left to the imagination of the players and the GM. Free to download as a PDF.[2]

Honey Heist
All of the players are bears. Their goal is to steal a load of honey from a fortress. The specifics are up to you, the Honey Master (HM). It's hilarious, fun and free from the creator's website.[3]

Lasers & Feelings
The players are in outer space on a ship called Raptor. The captain has had their mind taken over by a strange entity. It's up to the crew to save the day! Free to download.[4]

Lost in the Fantasy Worlds
A classic TTRPG premise that's a lot of fun: kids get sucked into a magical world while on a ride at an amusement park. They are each granted one magical power and must work together to find their way home! Free from Drive-Thru RPG.[5]

Online resources

2-Minute Tabletop

https://2minutetabletop.com

2-Minute Tabletop is a treasure trove of online maps, adventures and much more. Some items incur a cost but many are listed for free. I use this website on a weekly basis to find beautifully drawn maps that include caves, towns, forests and almost every kind of setting you can think of.

American Library Association (ALA): Games and Gaming Round Table

www.ala.org/rt/gamert

An amazing forum that exchanges ideas all about gaming in libraries.

Bits and Mortar

www.bits-and-mortar.com

A site that provides free PDFs of TTRPGs that you have purchased from a registered Bits and Mortar shop.

D&D: Basic Rules:

https://media.wizards.com/2018/dnd/downloads/DnD_BasicRules _2018.pdf

A simplified version of the D&D Player's Handbook, all free to download.

Dungeon Masters Guild

www.dmsguild.com

A huge array of (mainly D&D) adventures and guides, many free, some for a very reasonable price.

Drive-Thru RPG

www.drivethrurpg.com

Similar to the Dungeon Masters Guild but with a wide variety of TTRPG guides and adventures available.

Dungeon Vault

https://dungeonvault.com

A massive compilation of TTRPG puzzles, tokens and worlds.

Reddit RPG

www.reddit.com/r/rpg

Reddit has a bad reputation because, yes, I'm sure there are horrible things on there – but I've been a part of the TTRPG threads and communities and have found a very welcoming, friendly space. There are an endless well of ideas, maps and information available.

Roll20

https://roll20.net

Roll20 is an online platform that is free to use and hosts several
TTRPG formats. There is a bit of a learning curve, but it is a very
useful programme.

Sly Flourish

https://slyflourish.com

A one-stop shop for GMs everywhere. Primarily aimed at D&D, Sly
Flourish's website is crammed full of amazing ideas. These include
tips for building exciting games, encounters that will be remembered
for a long time and step-by-step guides on specific D&D campaigns.
Extremely useful and easy to read, a must-use.

Tabletop Audio

https://tabletopaudio.com

A free resource that does not require any installation of programs or
registration of any kind. The best thing about Tabletop Audio is that
you can find music based on themes. You can also download tracks
and store them for future use. If you are playing online, a program like
this can really add a lot of atmosphere and ambience to your game.

Recommended reading

The Game Master's Book of Non-Player Characters by Jeff Ashworth.
A very well-made resource for any GM who needs an NPC in a short
amount of time. These characters are fully fleshed out with their own
personalities and quirks. Great to build a believable, immersive world.

The Prepless Game Master by Paul Camp.
Eighty pages of resources for the GM who has no time to prep.
Practical advice on how to run a TTRPG with no preparation required
– essential reading!

Gaming in Libraries by Kelly Nicole Czarnecki.
A great book filled with practical, sound advice on setting up games of
all kinds in your library. It will help you set up a system that works for
your budget and your patrons. An essential read!

The Lazy Dungeon Master by Sly Flourish.
An essential guide for anyone hoping to be a GM but with little time.
The skills and practical tips provided can be applied to almost any
TTRPG. Very highly recommended.

*The Library as Playground: How Games and Play Are Reshaping Public
Culture* by David Leorke.
A brilliant reimagining of the public library space using games and
gaming as a template. The book illustrates how prevalent and
important gaming is to public libraries.

Table Fables: A Collection of Tables for the Weary Game Master by Madeline Hale.

No matter what TTRPG you play, your players will inevitably ask questions such as 'What does this corpse have on him?' or 'What's for sale in this shop?' This is an amazing book filled with random tables just for those kinds of questions. It will save you time and a ton of anxiety.

The Ultimate Micro RPG Book by James D'Amato.

Minimal set-up, fast paced and set in many different areas like outer space, dense jungles and eerie dungeons, this is a must-have for librarians with little time but a lot of demand for TTRPGs.

Fiction reading list for ages 9+

A Young Adventurer's Guide by Dungeons & Dragons (ages 9+).

This series covers multiple areas of D&D like monsters, spells, weapons, magical items, exotic locations and different classes. They are hugely popular in our library with a wide variety of ages.

The Dark is Rising by Susan Cooper (ages 9+).

Eleven-year-old Will is granted magical powers and must learn to harness them. A great introduction to the legend of King Arthur and full of really creepy, dark villains and atmospheric terror. But still great for ages nine and up.

The Book of Secrets by Alex Dunne (ages 9+).

When fairies come to the town of Clonbridge, everything changes, and not all for the better. A thrilling adventure with an amazing cast of characters.

Endless Quest by Matt Forbeck (ages 9+).

This is a fantastic choose-your-own-adventure series focusing on different aspects of D&D. Very popular and deserves a lot of attention.

Rules for Vampires by Alex Foulkes (ages 9+).

Hilarious, spooky and full of great illustrations, a book that will keep kids up at night and have them laughing out loud – don't miss it!

Mighty Jack by Ben Hatke (ages 9+).

A fun, touching and thrilling graphic novel adaptation of Jack and the Beanstalk. It's a wonderful series that deserves a lot of attention.

A Pinch of Magic by Michelle Harrison (ages 9+).

The three Widdershins sisters are trapped in their home until they locate three powerful magic items that will end the curse that keeps them there. This is a very popular series in our library.

Nura and the Immortal Palace by M. T. Khan (ages 9+).
Great for worldbuilding, it's a fantasy tale about a girl named Nura
who is whisked form modern-day Pakistan into the eerie, magical
world of the jinn. Nura must find a way to save her best friend and get
them all to safety.

The Legend of Podkin One-Ear by Kieran Larwood (ages 9+).
Magical story about a rabbit entrusted with a magical weapon that he
needs to use to save the world. A modern classic.

Tristan Strong Punches a Hole in the Sky by Kwame Mbalia (ages 10+).
Spending an entire month with relatives in Alabama is something
Tristan is not looking forward to. But when he's transported to a
mysterious world, all of his skills are put to the test. A fantastic
adventure with loads of historical African American heroes.

Mia and the Lightcasters by Janelle McCurdy (ages 9+).
Mia must learn to harness her new-found magic if she and her brother
are going to locate their missing parents. Heart-thumping action and
tons of great characters and monsters.

Time Villains by Victor Piñeiro (ages 9+).
When historical figures come to life, including Blackbeard the Pirate,
Javier and his little sister must harness his family's magical abilities to
save his town, and possibly the world.

Lightfall: The Girl and the Galdurian by Tim Probert (ages 9+).
A beautiful graphic novel about a girl whose grandfather goes missing.
To find him, she must embark on an epic quest that allies her with
strange and wonderful creatures. Hugely popular comic series for fans
of Amulet.

Knights of the Borrowed Dark by Dave Rudden (ages 11+).
When Denizen Hardwick discovers there are creatures that lurk and
thrive in the shadows, he is understandably worried. Then he
discovers he's part of a family of knights sworn to protect the world
from these creatures and must join an epic fight for humanity. A dark,
eerie series full of great action.

The Stowaway by R. A. Salvatore (ages 12+).
From the author who brought historic D&D characters to life (like
Drizzt Do'Urden), this fantasy pirate adventure is perfect for anyone
interested in playing TTRPGs.

Skandar and the Unicorn Thief by A. F. Steadman (ages 9+).
Skandar Smith only wants to be a unicorn rider, and just when his
dream is about to come true, the land's most powerful unicorn gets
stolen by a dark and ferocious enemy. Epic battles, ancient secrets,
loads here to glean for a great TTRPG session.

Nimona by Noelle Stevenson (ages 14+).
> A hilarious and deep story about shape-shifting Nimona, who teams up with Lord Blackheart to prove that a certain hero of the land isn't as nice as people think he is. A poignant graphic novel that should be on every school library shelf.

Shadow Chaser by Simon Tudhope (ages 10+).
> This is a unique choose-your-own-adventure TTRPG-style game book that allows you to create a character and explore a dark and sinister world.

Zachary Ying and the Dragon Emperor by Xiran Jay Zhao (ages 9+).
> Fans of Percy Jackson will devour this middle grade series, which is about a boy who must travel across China in order to close a portal to the underworld if he's going to save us all here on Earth. Hilarious and fast paced, not to be missed!

Notes

1   https://media.wizards.com/2015/downloads/dnd/MonsterSlayers_v3.pdf
2   www.wired.com/wp-content/uploads/blogs/geekdad/wp-content/uploads/2011/08/DnDish.pdf
3   https://gshowitt.itch.io/honey-heist
4   www.onesevendesign.com/laserfeelings
5   www.drivethrurpg.com/product/271653/Lost-in-the-Fantasy-World-Pamphlet-Edition

References

Camp, P. (2020) D&D Improv: The No-Prep Guide to DMing, *Dungeon Vault*, https://dungeonvault.com/dnd-improv-the-no-prep-guide-to-dming.

Forsythe, C. (2019) Roll for Initiative: A Player's Guide to Tabletop Role-Playing Games in Libraries, FIMS Publications. 343.

Kaylor, S. L. B. (2017) Dungeons and Dragons and Literacy: The Role Tabletop Role-playing Games Can Play in Developing Teenagers' Literacy Skills and Reading Interests, Graduate Research Papers. 215.

King, A. (2021) Why and How Dungeons & Dragons is so Good for Mental Health, *ScreenRant*, 3 March, https://screenrant.com/dungeons-dragons-mental-health-benefits-good-why-how.

Lear, K. (2022) The Mental Health Benefits of Dungeons & Dragons with Katie Lear, *You Should Have Been a Meat Shield*, season 1, episode 6, Buzzsprout, 22 June, https://bit.ly/3Q1SfaH.

Make a Skill Check (2021) D&D 5E: Beginner DM Tips, *Make a Skill Check*, 28 February, https://makeaskillcheck.com/new-dm-tips.

Oxendine, C. (2022) As an Autistic GM, Tabletop RPGs Provide a Perfect Structure for Social Interaction, *Dicebreaker*, 11 January. www.dicebreaker.com/categories/roleplaying-game/opinion/autistic-gm-tabletop-rpg-structure-social-interaction.

Preston, T. (2020) Kappan Authors on Play and Learning, *The Phi Delta Kappan*, **101** (8), 5–7.

Shea, M. (2019) Playing D&D Can Save Your Life, *Sly Flourish*, 16 December, https://slyflourish.com/playing_dnd_can_save_your_life.html.

Strang, R. (2022) An Interview With Rebecca Strang!, *You Should Have Been a Meat Shield*, season 1, episode 2, Buzzsprout, 8 June, https://bit.ly/3EmRia3.

Snow, T. (2019) Interesting Thing Happened after My Game Today, *Reddit*, www.reddit.com/r/DnD/comments/beg3n0/interesting_thing_happened_after_my_game_today.

Wright, J. C., Weissglass, D. E. and Casey, V. (2020) Imaginative Role-Playing as a Medium for Moral Development: Dungeons & Dragons Provides Moral Training, *Journal of Humanistic Psychology*, **60** (1), 99–129.

References

Index